First World War
and Army of Occupation
War Diary
France, Belgium and Germany

33 DIVISION
Divisional Troops
162 Brigade Royal Field Artillery
10 December 1915 - 11 June 1919

WO95/2413/4

The Naval & Military Press Ltd
www.nmarchive.com
Published in association with The National Archives

Published by

The Naval & Military Press Ltd

Unit 10 Ridgewood Industrial Park,

Uckfield, East Sussex,

TN22 5QE England

Tel: +44 (0) 1825 749494

www.naval-military-press.com

www.nmarchive.com

This diary has been reprinted in facsimile from the original. Any imperfections are inevitably reproduced and the quality may fall short of modern type and cartographic standards.

© **Crown Copyright**
Images reproduced by permission of The National Archives, London, England, 2015.

Contents

Document type	Place/Title	Date From	Date To
Heading	WO95/2413/4		
Heading	33rd Division Divl Artillery 162nd Brigade R.F.A. Dec 1915- Jun 1919		
Heading	33rd Division 162nd Bde R.F.A. Vol I Dec. 5 Jan. 9		
War Diary	Bulford Wills England	10/12/1915	11/12/1915
War Diary	Southampton	11/12/1915	11/12/1915
War Diary	Harve	12/12/1915	12/12/1915
War Diary	Railhead	13/12/1915	13/12/1915
War Diary	Mont Bernenchon Pas St. Venant Pas. De. Calais	14/12/1915	31/12/1915
Miscellaneous			
Heading	162nd Bde R.F.A. Vol 2		
War Diary	Mont Bernenchon Pas St. Venant Pas De Calais France	02/01/1916	31/01/1916
Heading	162 Bde R.F.A. 33 Div Vol 3 Feb 16		
War Diary	Mont Bernenchon	03/02/1916	27/02/1916
War Diary	Mont Bernenchon	14/02/1916	25/02/1916
War Diary		01/03/1916	31/03/1916
War Diary	Vermelles	09/03/1916	09/03/1916
War Diary	Vermelles Bethune	18/03/1916	26/03/1916
War Diary	Bethune	26/03/1916	28/03/1916
War Diary	Annequin	29/03/1916	31/03/1916
War Diary		16/03/1916	16/03/1916
War Diary	Annequin	02/04/1916	27/04/1916
War Diary	Beuvry	28/04/1916	28/04/1916
War Diary	Annequin	29/04/1916	17/05/1916
War Diary	Bethune	19/05/1916	19/05/1916
War Diary	Annequin	24/05/1916	24/05/1916
War Diary	Bethune	27/05/1916	27/05/1916
War Diary	Annequin	04/06/1916	04/06/1916
War Diary	Cuinchy	17/06/1916	17/06/1916
War Diary	Annequin	18/06/1916	18/06/1916
War Diary	Givenchy	20/06/1916	20/06/1916
War Diary	Annequin	20/06/1916	28/06/1916
Heading	War Diary Headquarters 162nd Brigade, R.F.A. (33rd Division) July 1916		
War Diary	Annequin	02/07/1916	07/07/1916
War Diary	Mont Bernenchon	09/07/1916	09/07/1916
War Diary	Longeau	10/07/1916	10/07/1916
War Diary	Soues	11/07/1916	12/07/1916
War Diary	Daours	13/07/1916	13/07/1916
War Diary	Treux	14/07/1916	14/07/1916
War Diary	Becordel Becourt	15/07/1916	15/07/1916
War Diary	Caterpillar Valley	16/07/1916	31/07/1916
Miscellaneous	Casualty List		
Miscellaneous	Casualties	03/08/1916	03/08/1916
Heading	33rd Divisional Artillery 162nd Brigade Royal Field Artillery August 1916		
War Diary		01/08/1916	28/09/1917
Miscellaneous	Casualties-September 1917		
War Diary		01/10/1917	31/10/1917
Miscellaneous	Casualties-October 1917		

Miscellaneous	5th Division No. G.B. 157	07/10/1917	07/10/1917
Miscellaneous	H.Q 33rd Divl Art	11/12/1917	11/12/1917
War Diary		01/11/1917	26/12/1917
Miscellaneous	Casualties	05/12/1917	05/12/1917
War Diary		01/01/1918	31/01/1918
War Diary		01/02/1918	28/02/1918
War Diary		01/03/1918	31/03/1918
Heading	33rd Divisional Artillery 162nd Brigade R.F.A. April 1918		
Miscellaneous	P/A With 162nd Brigade R.F.A. War Diary For April 1918		
War Diary		01/04/1918	28/04/1918
Miscellaneous	Note On Activities Of 162nd Bde. R.F.A. Sent By Colonel E.J. Skinner		
Miscellaneous	General Observations		
War Diary		01/05/1918	31/05/1918
War Diary		01/06/1918	30/06/1918
War Diary		01/07/1918	30/07/1918
War Diary		01/08/1918	01/09/1918
War Diary		01/09/1918	30/09/1918
War Diary		01/00/1918	30/10/1918
War Diary		01/11/1918	11/06/1919

WD95/2413 (4)

WD95/2413 (4)

33RD DIVISION
DIVL ARTILLERY

162ND BRIGADE R.F.A.
DEC 1915 - JUN 1919

162⁻ᵗᵉⁿ Bd.=Pfg.
Vol I

121/7911

33 ᵗᵉⁿ Division

Army Form C. 2118.

WAR DIARY
or
INTELLIGENCE SUMMARY.
(Erase heading not required.)

162nd Brigade R.F.A.

Instructions regarding War Diaries and Intelligence Summaries are contained in F. S. Regs., Part II. and the Staff Manual respectively. Title pages will be prepared in manuscript.

Place	Date	Hour	Summary of Events and Information	Remarks and references to Appendices
Bulford W. Wilts England	10/9/15	5.30 a.m.	Brigade Ammunition Column left Bulford Camp	
Do.	11/9/15	9.30 a.m. 3.30 p.m.	Batteries and Headquarter staff left Camp, Bulford	
Southampton		6.30 p.m.	Brigade left Southampton	
Havre	12/9/15		Brigade arrived at Havre, early morning Brigade left Havre for Railhead	
Railhead	13/9/15	5.15 p.m.	Brigade arrived at Railhead "B" & "C" Batteries at Thennes "A" Battery, Hearigny, "D" Battery & Ammunition Column at Ome	
		1 am	Headquarters to "A" Battery arrived and concentrated in Billets	
		3 am	"B" Battery " " " " "	
	14/9/15	5 am	Ammunition Column " " " "	
		11 am	"C" Battery " " " " "	
		12 am	"D" Battery " " " " "	
Do.	15/9/15		Information received that in certain events, Reserve Division of 10th Corps would concentrate. 162nd Brigade belonging to "A" Group of Reserve Division would march. Route was reconnoitred 15/9/15	

Army Form C. 2118.

WAR DIARY
~~INTELLIGENCE SUMMARY~~
(Erase heading not required.)

162nd Brigade R.F.A.

Place	Date	Hour	Summary of Events and Information	Remarks and references to Appendices
	16/12/15		33rd Div'l Arty letter Bm 97 of 16/12/15 received. Training of 33rd Divisional Artillery. To be carried out by 2nd Divisional Artillery with a view to the latter's relief by the 33rd Divisional Artillery at a later date. General Scheme:- (a) Half the Officers & half the No 1, Brigade & Battery Staffs to be attached to corresponding formations for 3 days, followed by the other half for a similar period. (b) Personnel of the 6.18 pr. & 2 Howitzer Sections to be subsequently attached to Batteries of 2nd Divisional Artillery for periods of 3 days until completed. (c) Arrangements to be made between Divisions for instruction in the duties of Divisional Ammunition Column & Headquarters, Divisional Artillery. (d) Arrangements to be made by 1st Corps for attachment of 1 man per Battery to No 22 Anti-Aircraft Battery for instruction in distinguishing between Allied & enemy aeroplanes.	
	17/12/15		Improvements to Billets & Horse Standings started by all Units.	
	18/12/15		33rd Divisional Artillery letter Bm/A/31 Copy No 2 Orders issued for Brigade to be formed temporarily into 6 Gun Batteries as follows. B/162 Brigade + Right half B/156 Brigade. B/162 " + Right half "A" 162 " C/162 " + Left half "A" 162 "	

Army Form C. 2118.

WAR DIARY
INTELLIGENCE SUMMARY
(Erase heading not required.)

162nd Brigade R.F.A.

Instructions regarding War Diaries and Intelligence Summaries are contained in F.S. Regs., Part II. and the Staff Manual respectively. Title pages will be prepared in manuscript.

Place	Date	Hour	Summary of Events and Information	Remarks and references to Appendices
	18/2/15	11.45 a.m.	Departure of 1st Party for attachment to 2nd Divisional Artillery as follows:— "D"/162 R.F.A. to 71st Battery } 2nd Div'l Arty. — 50th Battery } 1st Army Artillery Advanced "C"/A/162 — 16th Battery } Inspected Brigade. (signed) [illegible] H.Q. Staff	
PAS DE CALAIS, PAR LE VENANT. MONT BERNENCHON.	22/2/15	10.15 a.m.	Departure of 2nd Party for attachment to 2nd Divisional Artillery as follows:— "D" Battery 162 Brigade R.F.A. to 71st Battery } 2nd Div'l Arty. "B" " 162 " " 50th " " " " "C"&"A" " 162 " " 19th " " " 1st Corps advanced materials Bde. "C"&"A" Brigade Ann Col.	
	23/2/15		3 men from 18th Middlesex arrived as F.B. men to remain with unit until its departure for firing line. Lieut. C. J. Meakham and Lieut. R. J. Bamber posted to "A"&"D" Batteries respectively.	
	26/2/15		Departure of 3rd Party for attachment to 2nd Divisional Artillery as follows:— 1/c Bde. & Right Section "A" Battery 162 Bde. R.F.A. to 50th Battery } 2nd Div'l Right Section "B" Battery 162 Bde. R.F.A. to 71st Battery } Arty. Party from Bde. Ann. Col. to 36th Brigade Ann Col.	
	28/2/15		Saipion from R.E. attached temporarily to supervise workers in the work of improving hillis & horse standings. No. 75 Dr. J. Roath, HeP Staff, wounded at CAMBRIN, making the 1st Casualty of 162nd Bde. R.F.A.	

Army Form C. 2118.

WAR DIARY
INTELLIGENCE SUMMARY.
(Erase heading not required.)

162nd Brigade RFA

Place	Date	Hour	Summary of Events and Information	Remarks and references to Appendices
	30/10/16	10.15 am	# Reporting for the Party for attachment to 2nd Div'l Artillery preliminary to taking over Batteries. Right Section "A" Battery 162 Brigade to Battery } number & Left Section "A" Battery 162 Brigade to Battery } Right Section "B" Battery 162 Brigade to Battery } Arty. Party from Howitzer One to Howitzer Battery (Unknown) Also known for Battery for attachment to No 22 Anti-Aircraft Battery for instruction in observation between aeroplanes. Orderly Officer went up on this date.	
	31/10/16		The 99th Infantry Brigade to which 162nd Bde RFA is affiliated moved into BONNEHEM. The O/C 162 Bde RFA went over with the Brigade accommodated as connected Area for Reserve troops	

John Stephenson Carruthers
O/C 162 Bde RFA

Army Form C. 2118.

WAR DIARY
or
INTELLIGENCE SUMMARY.

(Erase heading not required.)

Instructions regarding War Diaries and Intelligence Summaries are contained in F. S. Regs., Part II. and the Staff Manual respectively. Title pages will be prepared in manuscript.

Place	Date	Hour	Summary of Events and Information	Remarks and references to Appendices

2353 Wt. W2514/1454 700,000 5/15 D. D. & L. A.D.S.S./Forms/C. 2118.

16 ad Poole, R.Ph.
Vol. 2

Army Form C. 2118.

WAR DIARY of 162nd Brigade R.F.A.
or
INTELLIGENCE SUMMARY.
(Erase heading not required.)

Jan: Vol 2.

Place: [illegible] Pas de Calais - Boran

Date	Hour	Summary of Events and Information	Remarks and references to Appendices
2		Chemical Adviser 1st Army saw Gas Demonstration in use of Gas Helmet.	
3		A Tactical Exercise was carried out to practice the supply of ammunition in conjunction with 99th Infantry Brigade. Party consisting of left sections "A" & "B" Batteries left for temporary attachment to 10th & 50th Batteries R.F.A., 2nd Div'l Arty.	
6		Brigade went Route March. C.R.A. 33rd Division interviewed Brigade Commanders regarding scheme for concentration of Reserve Division, 1st Corps.	
7		Party consisting of left sections of "C" & "D" Batteries left for temporary attachment to 16th & 71st Batteries, 2nd Div'l Arty.	
8		Instructions received to be ready to entrain at 9 hours notice between the period midnight 8/9th – midnight 15/16th.	
12		Brigade went route march with 99th Infantry Brigade. Capt H. Rhodes posted from Brigade Am. Col. to 33rd Divisional Am. Col. Capt W.L. Powrie posted to Brigade Am Col from 33rd Divisional Am Col.	
15		Farrier Sergeant posted from 87th Bde R.F.A.	
17		Shoeing Smith posted from No. 2 General Base.	

February 1916. WAR DIARY of 162nd Brigade R.F.A.   Army Form C. 2118.

INTELLIGENCE SUMMARY.

(Erase heading not required.)

Place	Date	Hour	Summary of Events and Information	Remarks and references to Appendices
	16		Farrier Sergeant posted.	
	18		5 Drivers posted. Instructions received that magazines of rifles of sentries (not in the front line of trenches) are to be charged, but no round is to be in the chamber. Safety catch to be kept at safety.	
	20		Lieuts G.J.A. Studdart & T.M. Howard posted. Sergeant G. Mitchell recommended for Commission.	
	21		Revised scheme of march table received to come into operation in the event of the 1st Corps line being broken.	
	22		9 Gunners & 3 Drivers posted from No. 2 General Base.	
	23		O/c Brigade submitted positions of Dismounted Cavalry Division for Reserve Scheme. O/c "B" & "R" Batteries submitted positions of Dismounted Cavalry Division for Reserve Scheme.	
	24			
	25		8 N.C.Os posted from 2nd Div l Arty to 162nd Brigade R.F.A. 8 N.C.Os posted to 2nd Div l Arty to form 162nd Brigade R.F.A.	

WAR DIARY of 162nd Brigade R.F.A.

February 1916

INTELLIGENCE SUMMARY
(Erase heading not required.)

Army Form C. 2118.

Place: Mont Bernenchon, Pas St Venant, Pas-de-Calais, France.

Date	Hour	Summary of Events and Information	Remarks and references to Appendices
25		Instructions received to place one Battery (less Officers & Gun detachments) at the disposal of 2nd Division & Battery to be at BETHUNE as soon after 11 am as possible & to draw into action at TOURBIERES. Battery detailed "C" Battery.	
26		33rd Div'l Arty inspected by 1st Corps Commander.	
27		"A" Battery & Right Section "A" Battery left to take over Gun positions of 17th Battery 2nd Div'l Arty in accordance with programme received 23-1-1916. Scheme received for the reinforcement either wholly or partially of the Artillery of the Right Division by the Artillery of the Reserve Division.	
29		6 Gunners posted from No. 2 General Base.	
30		On manoeuvres with 2nd, 12th & 33rd Divisions.	
31			

Signature: Lieut. Col. R.F.A.
Commanding 162nd Brigade R.F.A.

162. B2
R.F.a.
33 Des
Vol 3

Army Form C. 2118.

WAR DIARY of 162nd Brigade R.F.A.

INTELLIGENCE SUMMARY.

February 1916

(Erase heading not required.)

Instructions regarding War Diaries and Intelligence Summaries are contained in F.S. Regs., Part II. and the Staff Manual respectively. Title pages will be prepared in manuscript.

Place: Mont Bernenchon.

Date	Hour	Summary of Events and Information	Remarks and references to Appendices
3rd		Brigade went Route March. Map Reading Exercise for Officers & N.C.O.s carried out.	
4th			
8th		Brigade went Route March. 3 N.C.O.s from 2nd Div. Arty. Arty. bated.	
10th		2 Lieut. J.H.A. Student proceeded to LIETTRES on a course at 1st Army Artillery School.	
		The initial going into action of the 162nd Brigade R.F.A	
13th-14th		During the period 13th - 29th the 33rd Div. Arty. relieved the 12th Div. Arty. The 33rd Div. Arty. was, for tactical purposes, split into 2 Groups viz:- "A" & "Z". The 162nd Brigade R.F.A. went into action in the following manner:- "A" Battery placed at disposal of Heavy Artillery, 1st Corps for Counter Battery duty. (One detachment of C/162 took over Guns from "C"/63.	
23rd		Sections "B" & "D"/162 relieved Sections B/62 and C/62.	

13th-29th

February 1916. **WAR DIARY** of 162nd Brigade R.F.A.
INTELLIGENCE SUMMARY.
(Erase heading not required.)

Army Form C. 2118.
②

Place	Date	Hour	Summary of Events and Information	Remarks and references to Appendices
Thient Bermenchon	13-9 Feb		24th. 5 Signallers of Hqrs/162 took over "Z" Group. 6. P. Exchange. 25th. "B" "C" + D" /162 relieved Sections "C"/62, "C"/63 + "D"/162 respectively. 27th. Hqrs/162 + Amm Col /162 relieved Hqrs/65 + Amm Col /62 respectively.	
	14		Lieut. Col. J.A. Duncan attended 7th Army Artillery Course at AIRE	
	15		1 N.C.O. posted from 2nd Div. Arty. via 166th Bde R.F.A.	
	18		1 Gr + 2 Subs posted from No.2 General Base Depot.	
	21		1 Driver posted from 33rd Div. Arty. Headqrs.	
	23		1 Cpl posted proceeded to LIETTRES to attend 4th N.C.Os Course at 1st Army Artillery School 4 Subs + 2 Brs posted from No.2 General Base Depot	
	25			

Guy W Knutson Lieut. Col. R.A.
Commanding 162nd Brigade R.F.A.

Army Form C.2118.

WAR DIARY
INTELLIGENCE SUMMARY
(Erase heading not required.)

162nd Brigade R.F.A.   **March 1916.**

Instructions regarding War Diaries and Intelligence Summaries are contained in F.S. Regs., Part II. and the Staff Manual respectively. Title pages will be prepared in manuscript.

Place	Date	Hour	Summary of Events and Information	Remarks and references to Appendices
VERMELLES	1st to 31st		The Brigade still in action covering part of the 33rd Divisional Front composed of AUCHY SECTION & CUINCHY SECTION stretching from a point N.E. of VERMELLES to the LA BASSEE CANAL, held by the 19th, 98th, & 100th Infantry Brigades. O.C., 162nd Brigade R.F.A. took over the Command of AUCHY GROUP from O.C., 166th Brigade R.F.A. on 28th March. In this Group only one of the two Batteries of the Brigade originally in the Group remained i.e., "D" Battery. This Battery continued to (ly covered the extreme right of the Sector. "C" Battery which original covered the extreme left of AUCHY GROUP was transferred to CUINCHY GROUP remaining in the same position and with "B" Battery and "D" Battery 166th Brigade comprised the right sub-group, Commander by Major H.G.M.Johnston, "B"/162. "A" Battery continued to do counter-battery work attached to the XIth Corps Heavy Artillery and was at the disposal of the Group in the event of there being any need for wire-cutting. During the month "D" Battery from its position extreme N.W. of VERMELLES took part in a very successful raid into the enemy trenches made by the 1st Battalion Queen's Regiment, "A" Battery having cut the wire gap in the enemy wire preliminary to the raid.	
VERMELLES	9th		On March 9th the Officer's Mess of "D" Battery was destroyed by shell fire. This is the only Battery position of the Brigade which has been subjected to heavy shell fire but with this unit this is a very frequent occurrence. "D" Battery shelled with 15 cms shells. One shell fell in the Officer's Mess killing one and wounded two men who subsequently died from their wounds. 2nd Lieut R.S.S.Mitchell suffered from shell shock.	
VERMELLES BETHUNE.	18th 23rd		One Gunner wounded by shell fire. 2nd Lieut L.C.Hill took over duties of Adjutant from Lieut and Adjutant T.D.Shepherd transferred to the B.A.C.	
- do -	26th		Major O.M.Harris D.S.O., assumed Command of 162nd Brigade R.F.A vice Lieut-Colonel J.F.Duncan who left for England on the	

Army Form C. 2118.

162nd Brigade R.F.A.   MARCH 1916.   WAR DIARY / INTELLIGENCE SUMMARY

Instructions regarding War Diaries and Intelligence Summaries are contained in F.S. Regs., Part II. and the Staff Manual respectively. Title pages will be prepared in manuscript.

(Erase heading not required.)

Place	Date	Hour	Summary of Events and Information	Remarks and references to Appendices
BETHUNE	26th		continued. morning of the 27th. 2nd Lieut. C.J.Nathan proceeded to England and was struck off the strength.	
- do -	28th		162nd Brigade Headquarters removed to ANNEQUIN there forming the Headquarters of AUCHY GROUP 33rd DIVISIONAL ARTILLERY, Major O.M.Harris D.S.O., assuming command of the group.	
ANNEQUIN.	29th		One Gunner attached to R.E. Signals wounded by shell fire whilst patrolling lines.	
ANNEQUIN	30th		2nd Lieuts F.C.C.Manley and N.S.Bostock posted to "C" & "D" Batteries respectively.	
ANNEQUIN	31st		14093 Sergeant G.Mitchell proceeded to England to enter Cadet School preparatory to obtaining Commission in the Royal Field Artillery.	

SUMMARY.

CASUALTIES:
9-3-16 - "D" Batt { 14181 Gunner F.C.Coley (Cook). killed.
{ 14151 Bombdr J.Smith (Major Stewart's Servant) Died of Wounds.
{ 37212 Gunner A.Beard (Officer's Servant)   - do -
2nd Lieut R.S.S.Mitchell - shell shock.
"D" BATTY 63864 Gunner H.Dickson wounded 18-3-16.
"C" BATTY 13258 Gunner J.Owens wounded 29-3-16.

POSTINGS.
45093 Driver J.Howes to B.A.C.   ) 17-3-16 from No.2
112244 Driver W John to "D" Battery) General Base depôt.

120362 Gunner W.Stewart to "D" Battery) 23-3-16 from No.2.
1/2852 Gunner G.F.Steward to "A" Battery) General Base Depôt.
5859 Driver A.Lawrenson to "D" Battery)

48909 B.Q.M.S. W.Spaul promoted B.S.M. (on probation) and posted to "C" Battery from 156th Brigade R.F.A. - 28-3-16

162nd Brigade R.F.A.   **MARCH 1916.**

WAR DIARY
INTELLIGENCE SUMMARY

(Erase heading not required.)

Army Form C. 2118.

Place	Date	Hour	Summary of Events and Information	Remarks and references to Appendices
			SUMMARY continued. POSTINGS continued. 26912 Sergeant J.Langston "C" battery promoted B.Q.M.S. and posted to 166th Brigade R.F.A. Men admitted to hospital - 6. Men discharged to duty from hospital - 1. Rejoined from Reinforcements NAVES - 1. HORSES. Posted away - 11 (6 evacuated to M.V.S. and 5 to REMOUNTS GUNNERS. Joined - 12. Deaths - 4 (1 died : 3 killed(shot)). OMNavns Lieut-Colonel R.F.A. Commanding 162nd Brigade R.F.A.	

Army Form C. 2118.

MARCH 1916.   162nd Brigade R.F.A.,   **WAR DIARY**
or
INTELLIGENCE SUMMARY.

(Erase heading not required.)

Instructions regarding War Diaries and Intelligence
Summaries are contained in F. S. Regs., Part II.
and the Staff Manual respectively. Title pages
will be prepared in manuscript.

Place	Date	Hour	Summary of Events and Information	Remarks and references to Appendices

	16th		6 N.C.Os and men of "A" Battery accidentally wounded by explosion of a 5.9" German unexploded fuze which was being examined and taken to pieces by one of the N.C.Os. Names of wounded :-
			
			     13126 Sergt. F.G.Davis.
			     13142 Sergt. T.Humphreys.
			     13127 Sergt. W.J.Davis.
			     15463 Wheelr. A.L.Harris.
			     13076 Gunner W.Westwood.
			     13163 Gunner H.Quantrell.
			
			CASUALTIES - OFFICERS.
			
			2nd Lieuts R.S.S.Mitchell, A.P.Keable, and E.G.Attenborough appointed Lieutenants.
			2nd Lieut L.C.Hill appointed Lieutenant and appointed Adjutant vice lieut T.D.Shepherd to Regimental Duty.
			2nd Lieut T.R.Mayler (S.R). posted. to "B"/162.
			2nd lieut G.C.Carpenter admitted to Hospital 12th
			     Embarked for England from No. 2 Red Cross Hospital ROUEN 25th	

WAR DIARY
or
INTELLIGENCE SUMMARY.
(Erase heading not required.)

Army Form C. 2118.

MARCH 1916   162nd Brigade R.F.A.

Instructions regarding War Diaries and Intelligence
Summaries are contained in F. S. Regs., Part II.
and the Staff Manual respectively. Title pages
will be prepared in manuscript.

Place	Date	Hour	Summary of Events and Information	Remarks and references to Appendices
			P O S T I N G S.	
			To. From.	
		30851	To	
			77536 Dr. T.Bannister. H.Q.	
			110532 Dr. W.Barden. "C"	
			121268 Dr. J.H.Adams. "D"	
			113769 Dr. H.Carter. "D"	
			21578 Dr. W.Arman "C"	
			115762 Dr. F.Grice "C"	
			77450 Dr. Hodgson "D"	
			13337 Dr. J.Kirk. "A"	
			47914 Dr. R.Kenndy. H.Q.	
			9042 Dr. W.Knight. "D"	
			108095 Dr. Pinch. "D"	
			29387 Dr. Nicholas. "D"	
			95666 Dr. Paton H.Q.	
			15512 Dr. E.V.Zarrattini No. 2 General Base Depôt.	
			No. 2 General Base Depôt for transfer to England as under age ("A" Battery).	
			18 men admitted to hospital and evacuated from Div'l Area.	
			7 men wounded (6 accidental). (118th S.J.Lee).	
			16 men admitted to hospital and returned to duty without being evacuated.	
			Horses. 44 evacuated to M.V.S.	
			35 Joined.	
			5 rejoined from M.V.S.	
			4 deaths. (Accidental - drowned).	

M.M.McNairn   LIEUT. COLONEL, R.F.A.
COMMANDING 162nd BRIGADE, R.F.A.

Army Form C. 2118.

WAR DIARY
or
INTELLIGENCE SUMMARY
(Erase heading not required.)

162nd Brigade R.F.A.,

April May 1916.

Instructions regarding War Diaries and Intelligence Summaries are contained in F. S. Regs., Part II. and the Staff Manual respectively. Title pages will be prepared in manuscript.

Vol 8

XXIII
162 - RFA

Place	Date	Hour	Summary of Events and Information	Remarks and references to Appendices
	2nd		Brigade still in action on the front covered by the 33rd Division. All Batteries in the same positions as last month. Detachments from 39th Div. Arty attached for instruction.	
ANNEQUIN	15th	8.30 p.m.	A mine was sprung at MINE POINT on the AUCHY front. Artillery Bombardment from 8.30 p.m. to 9.30 p.m. to enable 2 officers and 50 men of 2nd Argyle and Sutherland Highlanders to raid the hostile trenches. The result was highly satisfactory.	
"	25th	10 p.m.	Artillery co-operated with 1st Battalion Middlesex Regt in a very successful raid carried out on the enemy trenches at MAD POINT. Two parties entered bayonetting two sentries and after bombing several dug-outs withdrew to our own lines bringing with them 3 unwounded prisoners of the 25th Reserve Jaeger Battalion. Our Artillery complimented and thanked by the G.O.C., 33rd Division.	
"	27th	5 a.m.	Heavy German Bombardment on front covered by the 16th Division followed by 2 Gas attacks at 6.30 a.m. and 8.30 a.m. - Wind being from South Easterly direction 33rd Divisional Artilx front got the gas and smoke helmets had to be worn for about half an hour in each attack. No casualties in Brigade.	
BEUVRY	28th		Wagon lines situated in BEUVRY shelled by 28 c.m. Howitzers. Several casualties in men and horses ixixxx of other Brigades but none in either "D"/162 and Headquarterstaff whose wagon lines are situated in the area shelled.	
	29th		No.1. HARLEY STREET (Field Dressing Station) shelled with 15 cm Howitzers, 10 direct hits out of 33 rounds fired. Shelling observed by aeroplane.	
			2 German aeroplanes brought down on this front.	

33
162 RFA
Vol 6

Army Form C. 2118.

162nd Brigade R.F.A., ~~MAY~~ JUNE 1916.

WAR DIARY
~~INTELLIGENCE SUMMARY~~

(Erase heading not required.)

Instructions regarding War Diaries and Intelligence Summaries are contained in F. S. Regs., Part II. and the Staff Manual respectively. Title pages will be prepared in manuscript.

Place	Date	Hour	Summary of Events and Information	Remarks and references to Appendices
ANNEQUIN	4th		The Brigade still in action holding a part of the 33rd Div'l Front. AUCHY Artillery Group Commanded by Lieut-Col O.M. Harris D.S.O.; Battery positions distributed from VERMELLES to LA BASSEE CANAL, 2 Batteries of this Brigade being in AUCHY GROUP, and 2 in CUINCHY GROUP.	
	11th	About 3.15 p.m.	Enemy shelled ANNEQUIN NORTH with 15 c.m. and 8" shells, searching for 60 Pounder Battery position on north side of LA BASSEE ROAD. The majority of shells fell short of the position and within 200 yards of AUCHY GROUP Telephone exchange. No artillery casualties. No material damage done.	
Do.	11th		AUCHY GROUP fired in support of 15th Division on receipt of S.O.S. Call. Enemy put up a heavy barrage of 7.7 c.m. 10.5 c.m. and 15 c.m. shells on 18 Pounder Battery positions in the TOURBIERES LOOP. VERMELLES, 4.5" Howitzers in ANNEQUIN NORTH, and again shelled the 60 Pounder position on north side of LA BASSEE ROAD with 8" and 15 c.m. shells. Altogether the barrage lasted for about 2 hours. Many lachrymatory shells were used. No material damage done and only one gunner casualty consisting of slight wound in the hand.	
Do.	13/14		"A" Battery, 162nd Brigade R.F.A., moved into position in TOURBIERES LOOP vacated by "C"/166 who went into training until May 23rd when they took over the Enfilade Section from "A"/167.	
Do.	15th	11 p.m.	Mine exploded S.E. of MIDNIGHT CRATERS A.27.b.60.95. Artillery bombardment of enemy trenches east and to flanks of this point whilst 16th K.R.R's raided enemy trenches. Shooting of Batteries very good. Corporal E.Williams, H.Q., injured by explosion of mine whilst on telephone duty in Boyau 20 with forward liason officer.	

Army Form C. 2118.

162nd Brigade R.F.A., MAY 1916. WAR DIARY

INTELLIGENCE SUMMARY.

(Erase heading not required.)

Instructions regarding War Diaries and Intelligence Summaries are contained in F. S. Regs., Part II. and the Staff Manual respectively. Title pages will be prepared in manuscript.

Place	Date	Hour	Summary of Events and Information	Remarks and references to Appendices
ANNEQUIN	17th	2.30 p.m.	Headquarters moved from ANNEQUIN to BETHUNE. 166th Brigade took over Group whilst Lieut-Col O.M.Harris, D.S.O., was on leave.	
BETHUNE.	19th		Re-organisation of Divisional Artillery. Each F.A.Brigade to consist of 3-18 pounders and 1-4.5" Howitzer Batteries. B.A.C's to merge into D.A.C's. "D"/162 posted to 167th Brigade becoming "B"/167. "C"/167 (How:) posted to 162nd Brigade becoming "D"/162 (How:) n 162nd B.A.C., merged into 33rd D.A.C., and known as No. 2 Section.	
ANNEQUIN	24th		22953 Corpl Kirby "D"/162 killed in action, by hostile fire.	
BETHUNE	27th	4.30 p.m.	Headquarters moved from BETHUNE to ANNEQUIN to take over AUCHY GROUP again from 166th Brigade R.F.A.,	

---oOo---

162nd Brigade R.F.A., MAY 1916. WAR DIARY

INTELLIGENCE SUMMARY.

(Erase heading not required.)

Place	Date	Hour	Summary of Events and Information	Remarks and references to Appendices
			CASUALTIES.	

Officers :-
2nd Lieut F.C.C.Manley attached X/33 T.M.B. 23-5-1916.
(Rejoined from Attachment to X/33 T.M.B. 23-5-1916.
2nd Lieut E.Parker Jones posted to No.22 A.A.Battery 20-5-16.
2nd Lieut G.E.L.Hancock posted from 33rd D.A.C., 20-5-16.

Men :-
Postings to Brigade :-   Postings from Brigade :-
2 Gunners, 1Driver & 1 Cold Shoer   1 Corpl to "D"/166.R.F.A.,
  from No. 2 G.B.Depôt.   1 Driver to "A"/166 R.F.A.
1 Cold Shoer, 3 Drivers & 1 Gunner   1 Gunner to No. 22 A.A.Bty.
  from /33rd D.A.C.;   1 B.S.M. to England on
1 Corpl from "H" Battery R.H.A.,   obtaining commission.
1 Corpl from 7th Bde R.H.A., A.C.,
1 Corpl from "D"/166 R.F.A.

Wounded :-
  22953 Corpl E.Kirby. (Subsequently died.).
  15390 Corpl E.Williams (in hospital 16 to 20th).
Sick :-   3 men (All evacuated from Div'l Area).   Joined :- 11 men.

Horses :-
Posted away :- 11 (7 to M.V.S., and 4 to 33rd Div'l Train).
Joined :-   25
Deaths :-   1 Destroyed: 2 Died.

O.McNamd Lieut-Col R.F.A.,
Commanding 162nd Brigade R.F.A.,

162 R.F.A.
Army Form C. 2118.
June
Vol 7

WAR DIARY
INTELLIGENCE SUMMARY
XXXIII

162nd Brigade R.F.A., JUNE 1916.

(Erase heading not required.)

Instructions regarding War Diaries and Intelligence Summaries are contained in F.S. Regs., Part II. and the Staff Manual respectively. Title pages will be prepared in manuscript.

Place	Date	Hour	Summary of Events and Information	Remarks and references to Appendices
ANNEQUIN	4th	11 p.m.	Batteries of AUCHY GROUP, R.A., bombarded enemy front trenches and support lines east of QUEEN'S CRATER for 35 minutes in support of raid made by the CAMERONIANS. One prisoner was taken:28 of the enemy were killed.	
CUINCHY	17th		"C"/162 gun position moved from CUINCHY GROUP R.A. to GIVENCHY GROUP R.A.,	
ANNEQUIN	18th		Enemy anti-aircraft shell exploded in Officer's Mess. No casualties.	
GIVENCHY	20th		"C"/162 new gun position heavily bombarded. Casualty :- Lieut D.B.Vick wounded.	
ANNEQUIN			"A"/162 gun position moved from AUCHY GROUP R.A.; to GIVENCHY GROUP R.A.,	
ANNEQUIN			AUCHY GROUP R.A., to be known in future as CUINCHY RIGHT SUB-GROUP.	
"	26th		Brigade Batteries in CUINCHY RIGHT Sub Group, Cuinchy Group, and GIVENCHY GROUPS commenced in conjunction with other batteries along the whole British Front 7 days bombardment consisting of shelling of enemy front line, support and communition trenches Back Areas and Wire cutting.	
"	28th		Batteries of CUINCHY RIGHT SUB GROUP R.A.,bombarded enemy trenches in the vicinity of MAD POINT., in support of raid made by Glasgow Highlanders (H.L.I). 2 mine shafts were destroyed. 46 prisoners were taken. Besides these prisoners one German Officer and 8 men are known to have been killed and 7 wounded. In addition several dug-outs containing Germans not included in the above totals were bombed.	

Army Form C. 2118.

162nd Brigade   JUNE 1916.

WAR DIARY
or
INTELLIGENCE SUMMARY

(Erase heading not required.)

Place	Date	Hour	Summary of Events and Information	Remarks and references to Appendices
			CASUALTIES.	
	1st.		Lieut D.B.Vick posted from Details 33rd D.A.C., to "C"/162 2nd Lieut F.C.C.Manley posted from C/162 to H.T.M.Battery (33rd Div.)	
	20th.		Lieut D.B.Vick wounded in action.	
	5th		16434 Corpl E.Oliver from Details 33rd D.A.C., to "D"/162	
	6th (		1977 Gr. W.J.O.Berwick - do - - do -	
	(		21023 Dr. J.Smart - do - - do -	
	(		6381 Dr. G.Kettle - do - - do -	
	7th (		6284 Gr. A.J.Albertson.) posted from 156th Bde R.F.A.,	
	(		22690 Gr. J.Brennan) to "A"/162 and H.Q/162 respectively	
	19th		24846 Sergt C.W.Hodgson from No. 2 G.B.Depôt.	
			6 men admitted to hospital (4 evacuated from Div8L Are a	
			4 men rejoined from Hospital.	
			5 horses evacuated to M.V.S.,	
			1 horse Died.	
			9 horses posted away.	

  [signature]
  Lieut-Col R.F.A.,
  Commanding 162nd Brigade R.F.A.,

Headquarters,

162nd BRIGADE, R.F.A.

(33rd Division)

J U L Y

1 9 1 6

Attached:
Casualty List.

Army Form C. 2118.

33 July
162 RFA
Vol 8

WAR DIARY
or
INTELLIGENCE SUMMARY.

162nd BRIGADE R.F.A., JULY 1916.

Place	Date	Hour	Summary of Events and Information
ANNEQUIN	2nd	12.15 a.m.	Artillery bombardment in support of raid made by "Worcester's" on enemy's trenches near RAILWAY CRATER following the explosion of two mines, one at MINE POINT and the other near RAILWAY CRATER. Artillery put a barrage round the raided area which inculded the enemy's support line. The enemy also put a barrage which was of no avail. The raiding party remained in the enemy's trenches for an hour and a quarter, blew up three mine shafts, in one of which were some of the enemy, two machine gun emplacements were destroyed and many dug-outs were bombed. The damage to the enemy's trenches was very considerable, and it is thought that at least 20 Germans were killed and many wounded. 13 prisoners were brought back, of whom three were killed by the enemy's fire when coming over. Our casualties were slight.

Army Form C. 2118.

162 BRIGADE R.F.A.,   **JULY 1916.**   **WAR DIARY** or **INTELLIGENCE SUMMARY**

(Erase heading not required.)

Instructions regarding War Diaries and Intelligence Summaries are contained in F. S. Regs., Part II and the Staff Manual respectively. Title pages will be prepared in manuscript.

Place	Date	Hour	Summary of Events and Information	Remarks and references to Appendices
ANNEQUIN	7th		Brigade left ANNEQUIN, marched to MONT BERNENCHON the same evening where it remained in billets until 9th inst.	
MONT BERNENCHON	9th		Entrained at CHOQUES en route for the south to take part in advance north of the SOMME. Detrained at LONGEAU: Headquarters, "A" & "B" Batteries and ¼ Section 33rd D.A.C., proceeded by road to CARDONETTE (about 6 miles N.E., of AMIENS) where they billeted for the night.	
LONGEAU	10th		"C" & "D" Batteries detrained at LONGEAU and marched to SOUES, south of the SOMME and about 15 miles W.N.F. of AMIENS where they were joined by Headquarters, "A" & "B" Batteries and ¾ Section D.A.C.;	
SOUES	11th		Rested at SOUES in billets.	
do	12th		Left SOUES as Brigade with No. 2 Section D.A.C.; and marched with rest of 33rd Div. Arty via AILLY and AMIENS to DAOURS a distance of about 20 miles. Bivouacked there night of 12th and 13th.	
DAOURS	13th		Left DAOURS about 8 a.m. and marched with rest of Div. Arty to a point just outside TREUX arriving there about midday and bivouacking there on top of hill.	
TREUX	14th		Received orders at 1.30 a.m. to harness up and stand by ready to move off. Moved off 3.30 a.m. with rest of Div. Arty arriving at MEAULTE about 7 miles from the firing line about 6 a.m. Halted there until about 11 a.m. when Brigade moved on to bivouac just in rear of BECORDEL-BECOURT. At about 4.30 p.m. C.O.; rode on to valley running E & W between MAMETZ and CATERPILLAR Woods North of MONTAUBAN to reconnoitre gun positions	
BECORDEL BECOURT			Wagon lines established immediately west of BECORDEL-BECOURT. Wagon lines shelled.	
do	15th		At 4.30 a.m. Batteries moved off independantly to take up positions on ridge in valley reconnoitred the previous day, "D"/162 (Howitzers) taking up a position about 1½ miles west of 18 pounders. At 8.30 a.m. Brigade took part in bombardment of German SWITCH LINE Trench reaching back to MARTINPUICH about 500 yards in rear. Bombardment lasted for one hour when fire was lifted on to MARTINPUICH and continued at slow rate. 98th Infantry Brigade	

2355 Wt.W2514/1454 700,000 5/15 D.D.&L. A.D.S.S./Forms/C.2118.

Army Form C. 2118.

WAR DIARY
or
INTELLIGENCE SUMMARY

162nd BRIGADE R.F.A., JULY 1916.

Sheet 2.

(Erase heading not required.)

Instructions regarding War Diaries and Intelligence Summaries are contained in F. S. Regs., Part II. and the Staff Manual respectively. Title pages will be prepared in manuscript.

Place	Date	Hour	Summary of Events and Information	Remarks and references to Appendices
Caterpillar valley.	16th		reached their objective but 100th Infantry Brigade were held up by flanking machine gun fire. Remainder of the day was spent in establishing communications between Headquarters and Batteries, Headquarters and Infantry Brigade, and Batteries and O.P's. O.P's taken up on top of ridge about 1 mile in front of Batteries in late German second line trenches. Headquarters established in strong German dug-out on corner of MONTAUBAN road where it meets the valley. During night 15th/16th SWITCH TRENCH was kept under heavy fire and ground from this trench back to MARTINPUICH and the village itself swept and searched at frequent intervals.	
do	17th		Wire cutting in front of SWITCH TRENCH and completeing registration of zones. Night firing as on 15th/16th.	
do	18th		Carried on previous day's programme. Night firing as on 16th/17th	
do	19th		Programme same as previous day. Headquarters and neighbourhood heavily shelled with lachrymatory shells from about 10 a.m. to 1 p.m. One direct hit on H.Q., dug out. No material damage done.	
do	20th		About 2.55 a.m. bombardment commenced preparatory to attack on HIGH WOOD by 15th Corps at 3.25 a.m. Our fire concentrated on HIGH WOOD. First lift at 3.25 a.m. Second at 3.35 a.m. on to final barrage line. Final barrage was established and continued for one hour after which ordinary night programme was resumed. Assault successful. HIGH WOOD taken. Towards evening however after being heavily shelled the whole day Infantry had to retire from the wood falling back on their original line on road running in front of BAZENTIN-LE-GRAND. During the whole day our 18 pounders kept intermittent fire on ground and roads leading into FLERS and FAUCOURT-ABBAYE. Barrage put up behind wood for about ½ an hour during retirement of our troops from HIGH WOOD.	
do	21st		Night firing to consist of 500 Rounds 18 pounders. 75-4.5" Howitzers. Zones moved to East of HIGH WOOD. Whole Division skide-slipped to right. During the day carried out registrations on new zones and kept up intermittent fire on part of SWITCH TRENCH occupied. Our infantry reported as once again holding southern half of	

Army Form C. 2118.

162nd BRIGADE R.F.A., JULY 1916   WAR DIARY or INTELLIGENCE SUMMARY.   Sheet 3.

Instructions regarding War Diaries and Intelligence Summaries are contained in F.S. Regs., Part II. and the Staff Manual respectively. Title pages will be prepared in manuscript.

(Erase heading not required.)

Place	Date	Hour	Summary of Events and Information	Remarks and references to Appendices
HIGH WOOD.			33rd Division Infantry relieved night of 21/22 by 51st Division composed of 153rd, 154th, & 155th Brigades. 33rd Div. Arty remained in Action to support 51st Division, 154th Brigade supported by 162nd Bde R.F.A., Starting at about 10 a.m. corner of MONTAUBAN ROAD and southern slope of Valley incessantly shell'd by 10-5 c.m and 15 c.m shells including many lachrymatory shells in the afternoon, Whole of valley from LONGUEVAL and either slope of valley shelled during the afternoon, shelling coming from enfilade from direction of FLERS and area between FLERS and DELVILLE WOOD. Night firing same as previous night except that no H.E. was allowed.	
	22nd		Short concentrated bombardment on SWITCH TRENCH beginning at 3.30 a.m and finishing at 3.30 a.m. 18 pdrs 2 rds per gun per min: 4.5" Hows 1 rd per gun per min. This expenditure to come out of night's allotment. Received orders early morning to register Bds on SWITCH TRENCH by aeroplane at 3.30 a.m. All batteries stood by ready but no aeroplane arrived to carry out registration. At 10.45 a.m. received orders to register N.W. corner of HIGH WOOD accurately. This was carried out by Batteries by 12 midday At about 1.50 p.m. received orders to bombard with 150 rounds 4.5" Hows; M.G's and dug-outs to west of HIGH WOOD. This was in conjunction with 59th Siege Battery(6"Hows) These machine guns reported to be holding up whole situation. At about 3.45 p.m eneny opened up a barrage on open spaces in front of the two BAZENTINS, area due west of HIGH WOOD and heavy barrage on CATERPILLAR WOOD; gradually slackened and eventually ceased at 4.30 p.m. At 7 p.m XV, XIII, & III Corps opened up a combined bombardment of supposed enemy front line defences and back areas preliminary to attack by infantry of the other Corps, 5th Div. on our right, 19th Div. on our left. Objective alloted to 51st Div. covered by 33rd Div. Arty N.E. & N.W. edges of HIGH WOOD and SWITCH TRENCH,	

Army Form C. 2118.

162nd BRIGADE R.F.A.,   JULY 1916.   Sheet. 4.

WAR DIARY
or
INTELLIGENCE SUMMARY
(Erase heading not required.)

Instructions regarding War Diaries and Intelligence Summaries are contained in F.S. Regs., Part II. and the Staff Manual respectively. Title pages will be prepared in manuscript.

Place	Date	Hour	Summary of Events and Information	Remarks and references to Appendices
	23rd		East and West, 162nd Bde to cover 154th Infantry Brigade. Ammn. allotment for 162nd Bde 20 rds per gun per hour up to 8 mins before Zero 1.30 a.m 25rd inst. When fire was increased to an increased rate. About 1.27 a.m Howitzer fire searched back by short lifts for 200 yards and then ceased. At 1.30 a.m 18 pdrs search back for 200 yards by short lifts and continued to search the ground for 300 or 400 yards back at frequent intervals until about 2 a.m when it slowed down again to 20 rds per gun per hour, gradually decreasing rate of fire until about 8 a.m when cease firing was given. Assault failed all along the line. Some of the objectives were gained and held for time but owing to machine gun fire infantry were held up on portions of line compelling successful units to fall back. Net result 6.0 a.m Corps holding same line as prior to attack. During the day the shelling of the valley was normal. Night firing consisted of 160 rds per Bde on DITCH TRENCH searching back behind the crest at frequent intervals. The Howitzer Batty Battery ordered not to fire at all until further orders. Owing to shortage of running out springs in j. A.G., only 6 of the 12 18 pdrs guns in the Bde were in action, two of these having to be pushed up before the guns could be fired again.	
	24th		At 5.50 a.m enemy opened up a very heavy fire with 7.7, 10.5, 15, and a few 21 c.m. shells. He bombardment started on the northern slopes of the valley itself and then up the southern slopes. This repeated at 7 a.m. and again in a minor degree at about 8.30 a.m. In each case the bombardment lasted for about 30 to 40 minutes. Thus we received no material damage and total casualties were 1 killed and 6 slightly wounded. At noon orders were received to the effect that 51st Div. Arty would take over the support of their own infantry from 33rd Div. Arty the latter to become Corps Artillery and to be responsible for whole front of XVth Corps in case of any enemy counter-attack, for searching hollows and back areas and for switching on to any part of XVth Corps front where fire might be needed.	

162nd BRIGADE R.F.A.,   JULY 1916.   WAR DIARY or **INTELLIGENCE SUMMARY**

Sheet 5.

(Erase heading not required.)

Army Form C. 2118.

Place	Date	Hour	Summary of Events and Information	Remarks and references to Appendices
			This entailed the moving of 18 pounder batteries which could not get a sufficient switch to the right from their original positions. For moving "A" & "B" Batteries further up the slope the same area was kept and registration on LONGUEVAL was carried out that afternoon. New O.P's in front of LONGUEVAL were reconnoitred. The right of Corps front running through Southern half and of DELVILLE WOOD and north of LONGUEVAL up to HIGH WOOD. 162nd Bde was made responsible for the right half together with -67th Brigade each covering and supporting the other.	
	25th		18 pounder batteries badly shelled suffering some casualties, "C"/162 escaping lightly compared with "A" & "B" Batteries. Several 8" Shells arrived in the middle of the two latter batteries during the day fortunately doing no damage to the guns. Night firing 24/25 750 rds per Brigade. 162nd Bde's task to pay special attention to HIGH WOOD also west corner of sunken wood from west corner for 300 yds S.W. and retrenchments N.W of this corner. Still only 6-18pdrs in action. Zone to be covered by the Brigade from about 250 yards inside N.W. corner of DELVILLE WOOD to about 600 yards N.W. Registration carried out on points in this zone and communications established to O.P's.	
	24th (cont)		At about 9 p.m enemy counter attack at LONGUEVAL and DELVILLE WOOD. 162nd Brigade Batteries switched over on to that zone when S.O.S. was received and gave a quick barrage. At about 9 p.m heavy shell either 15 or possible 22 c.m. fell on to dug-out in which 12 signallers and orderlies of H.Q., staff were sleeping. 10 of these were buried but after 3 hours work were dug out having received no injuries, the frame work having saved them from being completely buried. Enemy counter attack failed, all quiet being reported at about 12 midnight.	
	25th (cont)		Night firing 25th/26th same as previous night except for zones which were as quoted above in LONGUEVILLE DELVILLE WOOD area.	

Army Form C. 2118.

162nd BRIGADE R.F.A., JULY 1916.

WAR DIARY
or
INTELLIGENCE SUMMARY.
(Erase heading not required.)

Sheet 6.

Place	Date	Hour	Summary of Events and Information	Remarks and references to Appendices
	26th		At 1.30 a.m. orders received for bombardment at 6.10 a.m for one hour. Area to be bombarded in conjunction with 5th Div.Arty and Heavy Arty - DELVILLE WOOD & LONGUEVAL Village - last 5 minutes to be intense. This was carried out successfully and registration on LONGUEVAL was resumed. No. of guns in action - 5. At about 7 p.m a wireless induction set was installed in order to keep communications going when lines failed. At about 9 p.m the enemy opened up a barrage of K-Stoff gas shells. into the valley keeping it up until about 2 a.m 27th. Helmets were worn and there were a few casualties. One Corporal has since died from effects. At 4 p.m. orders received for bombardment in support of attack XV & XIII Corps on 27th. Objectives :- (a). Strong points in the orchards north of LONGUEVAL. (b). The village of LONGUEVAL. (c). DELVILLE WOOD. Divisions attacking - 2nd Div of XIII Corps on the right: 5th Div of XV Corps on the left. Bombardment to open 2 hours before Zero. Zero hour 7.10 a.m. At Zero bombardment to lift and a succession of barrages formed. Attack to be carried out in the form of a methodical progression from point to point under cover of artillery barrage. Final line to be orchard and enclosure north of LONGUEVAL and the line of the road running westwards. Task for 162nd Bde R.F.A., was to search and sweep the whole of this area the Southern boundary of the Bde lifts being always one lift in front of the area to be attacked. Fire to be intense for 7 minutes prior to each of the three lifts. Rate of fire for 18 pounders 1st hour 1¾ rds per gun per min. Afterwards one round per gun permin: 4.5" Hows: 1st hour 1 round per How: per min: Afterwards 1 round per How: per 1½ minutes.	
	27th		Operation orders of previous day carried out at 8.10 a.m Brigade resumed its ordinary work except that batteries searched approaches more actively whilst consolidation was in progress. Result of combined attack - the right gained objectives - the left held up at points. Sharp fighting continued during the day, coming to a climax at	

Army Form C. 2118.

162nd BRIGADE R.F.A.   JULY 1916.   WAR DIARY
                                          or
                        Sheet 7.   INTELLIGENCE SUMMARY
                                    (Erase heading not required.)

Instructions regarding War Diaries and Intelligence
Summaries are contained in F. S. Regs., Part II
and the Staff Manual respectively. Title pages
will be prepared in manuscript.

Place	Date	Hour	Summary of Events and Information	Remarks and references to Appendices
	28th		about 6 p.m when the enemy counter-attacked putting up a very heavy barrage of all calibres from 7.7 c.m to 22 c.m on LONGUEVAL and DELVILLE WOOD. This was successfully repulsed by our troops in conjunction with our artillery. At about 9.30 a.m a 15 c.m shell fell into large pit in rear of "B" Battery position where men's breakfast was being cooked resulting in the deaths of the B.S.M. & 4 men and one Sergt. suffering from Shell Shock. Night firing 27/28 same as previous night.	
	29th		A quiet day. Usual searching and sweeping of hollows and back areas in support of infantry who successfully consolidated points gained in LONGUEVAL and DELVILLE Woods in spite of their being subjected to heavy fire at intervals during the night. Night firing orders same as night 27/28. Orders received about 12.30 p.m for bombardment to commence at 3 p.m and to last until 3.30 p.m. Zone allotted to 162nd Bde part of SWITCH TRENCH about midway between and N.E., of HIGH & DELVILLE WOODS. This in preparation for further operations on 30th. 17 guns now in action and night firing consisted of same targets as 28/29 but allotment of 750 rds per Bde.	
	30th		At about 2.30 a.m the Germans again opened up a slow fire of K-Stoff gas shells on to the valley sweeping and searching. Weather being very misty particularly suitable to his purpose & the gas hung about for about 2½ hours. Gas helmets were worn and casualties averted. About 3.15 a.m bombardment on same lines as the previous day opened up and continued until 5.15 a.m. Ammunition allowance 60 rds per gun & How: Heavy artillery to be particularly active on hostile batteries in a line HIGH WOOD - FLERS - GUEUDECOURT to assist XIIIth Corps. Favourable news received in the morning as to infantry consolidation. Orders received about 12.30 p.m for bombardment in support of attack by XVth Corps on sunken road from N.W face of DELVILLE Wood to Eastern corner of HIGH Wood inclusive of strong enemy post at latter point. Task allotted to 162nd Bde to bombard central portion of German SWITCH Trench situated about 800 yards in rear of road, to be attacked. Fire to be increased to as	

"Caterpillar Valley.	29th	On the afternoon of the 29th whilst Caterpillar Wood to the rear of "D" Battery was being shelled some unlucky shots fell on the Battery position, one direct hit being obtained on one of the guns which was completely buried. An ammunition limber was flung into the air; all the rounds were scattered round at an average radius of 100 yards, but not one detonated. Casualties among the gun detachment were 5 killed and one wounded.

-----------O o O-----------

Army Form C. 2118.

162nd BRIGADE R.F.A.,   JULY 1916.   WAR DIARY
                                            or
                          INTELLIGENCE SUMMARY.
Sheet 8.
(Erase heading not required.)

Instructions regarding War Diaries and Intelligence
Summaries are contained in F. S. Regs., Part II.
and the Staff Manual respectively. Title pages
will be prepared in manuscript.

Place	Date	Hour	Summary of Events and Information	Remarks and references to Appendices
	31st		intense a rate as possible at 7 mins to Zero and to continue firing on SWITCH Trench for 30 mins after Zero gradually slowing down and stopping when no longer required. Zero hour 6.10 p.m Bombardment to commence at 4.45 p.m. Ammn allotment 18 pdrs - 100 rds per gun - 4.5" Hows: 100 rds per gun increased from 100 to 200 rds per gun at 4 p.m in case of 18 pdrs. Result of attack obscure for some time. Night firing continued as usual except that a double zone had to be dealt with by the Bde viz: a protective zone on SWITCH TRENCH and the usual searching fire on back areas just to the north of LONGUEVAL and DELVILLE Wood. Enemy attempted two counter attacks during night 30/31 niether of which were successful. Situation report received early in morning to the effect that the situation still rather obscure. XIIICorps successful in reaching their objectives but right of XVth Corps held up by enemy machine gun fire from strong posts in enclosure to north of LONGUEVAL orchards. Same reported on the left viz: East corner of HIGH Wood. Infantry reached objective namely sunken road running from East corner of HIGH Wood down to LONGUEVAL but were "Krumped" out of it and had to retire on to original line. Day firing consisted of the usual sniping and keeping bursts of searching fire on roads, hollows and back areas. Very little shell fire at all on any gun positions. Night firing 31st July/1st August same as previous night, half guns being kept laid on protective zone (S.O.S Zone) and half on usual night lines in rear of SWITCH TRENCH.	

---------- 30c ----------

CASUALTY LIST.

Army Form C. 2118.

62nd BRIGADE R.F.A., JULY 1916. WAR DIARY or INTELLIGENCE SUMMARY

Sheet 9.

(Erase heading not required.)

Place	Date	Hour	Summary of Events and Information	Remarks and references to Appendices
			CASUALTIES.	

Killed or Died of Wounds.

    1 Officer.   21 Other Ranks.

Wounded and evacuated.

    8 Officers.   48 Other Ranks.

Wounded - remained at or returned to Duty.

    2 Officers.   4 Other Ranks.

Posted to Brigade. - Reinforcements.

    8 Officers.   45 Other Ranks.

OFFICER CASUALTIES.

    Headquarters.

    2nd Lieut. R.A.Jacobs - Wounded & evacuated 21-7-1916.

"A" Battery.

2nd Lieut V.Hailey - Wounded & evacuated 16-7-1916.
2nd Lieut N.K.Brookes - Posted 29-7-1916.

"B" Battery.

Lieut A.P.Keable - Gassed 24th Evacuated 27th
2nd Lt. N.S.Bostock - Wounded 15th (remained at Duty)
Lt. T.D.Shepherd - Posted 29th

Army Form C. 2118.

162nd BRIGADE R.F.A.,   JULY 1916.   WAR DIARY or INTELLIGENCE SUMMARY.

Sheet 10.

Place	Date	Hour	Summary of Events and Information	Remarks and references to Appendices
			Casualties continued.	

"C" Battery.

2nd Lieut. H.C.Osborne - Wounded & evacuated 15-7-1916.
Lieut C.Moore - Wounded & evacuated 21-7-1916.
2nd Lieut. H.E.Fisher - Wounded and evacuated 30-7-1916.
2nd Lieut. P.Strachan - Posted 24-7-1916.
2nd Lieut. L.E.Fisher - Posted 29-7-1916.
2nd Lieut B.S.M.Paterson - Posted 31-7-1916.

"D" Battery.

Major W.P.Bennett. - Killed in action 15-7-1916.
Major Lieut W.D.Watson - Wounded (1st) 16-7-16 Remained at Duty.
                         Wounded (2nd) & evacuated 21-7-16.
2nd Lieut G.E.L.Babcock - Wounded & evacuated 18-7-1916.
Capt. T.St.P.Bunbury - Posted 17-7-1916.
Lieut. A.E.G.Champion - Posted 24-7-1916.
2nd Lieut A.G.Walton - Posted 27-7-1916.
2nd Lieut F.H.Warr - Wounded(Gassed) 27-7-16. Returned to Duty 30-7-1916.

3/8/16

M.Norris
Lieut-Col R.F.A.,
Commanding 162nd Brigade R.F.A.,

33rd Divisional Artillery

162nd BRIGADE

ROYAL FIELD ARTILLERY

AUGUST 1 9 1 6

Army Form C. 2118.

WAR DIARY
or
INTELLIGENCE SUMMARY.
(Erase heading not required.)

162 Bde RFA Vol 9

Place	Date	Hour	Summary of Events and Information	Remarks and references to Appendices
	1916. August. 1st.	5.30 a.m.	Order received to the effect that 162nd & 166th Brigades would be relieved by 78th & 79th Brigades 17th Division, respectively, and would proceed to Wagon Lines at BECORDEL BECOURT, then to 78th & 79th Wagon Lines at DERNANCOURT. Relief to take place between 4 p.m. and 7 p.m. D/78 came up to D/162 position whilst 4 German planes were over the position with the result that 5.9's and 4.2's and 4" H.V. were poured on to the Battery Position blowing in one dug-out, and resulting in 2 horses killed, one Driver killed and one missing. Soon after "D" Battery had left Gun position one of the Ammunition dumps was blown up by shell fire. Relief completed about 9 p.m. New Wagon Lines established by 2.30 a.m. 2nd instant.	
	2nd to 11th		Period from 2nd to 11th instants, spent in rest at DERNANCOURT. Wagon Lines left by former Units in very untidy condition, entailing much work during our period of rest in building incinerators and carting away several weeks accumulation of rubbish and manure and putting lines generally in a sanitary condition. In this great assistance was received from the working parties provided by A.D.M.S. 33rd Division. Owing to shortage of material for necessary repairs to Guns in action - especially in running out springs - and the general unsatisfactory experience of the 18 pounder Buffer during prolonged bombardments, Orders were received on 9th instant to the effect that Guns and accessories of Brigades in the Lines would be kept up to strength by those in rest.	
	11th		Orders received on evening of 10th instant to relieve 156th and 167th Brigades which had been in action on LONGUEVAL - HIGH WOOD front from 15th July without rest. On this date 162nd & 166th Batteries marched independently to relieve 167th & 156th Brigades, respectively followed Wagon Lines of all Brigades mutually exchanged.	

Army Form C. 2118.

WAR DIARY
or
INTELLIGENCE SUMMARY.
(Erase heading not required.)

Instructions regarding War Diaries and Intelligence Summaries are contained in F. S. Regs., Part II. and the Staff Manual respectively. Title pages will be prepared in manuscript.

Place	Date	Hour	Summary of Events and Information	Remarks and references to Appendices
	1916. August 11th.		162nd Brigade after reconnaissance on 9th instant by O.C., Brigade and Battery Commanders' took up positions as follows:- B/162 & C/162 forming two six Gun Batteries, under the Command of Major R.G.M.Johnston and Capt: A.B.VanStraubenzee, respectively, with 2 Subalterns and detachments of A/162 attached, in positions in a sunken part of the Southern slope of CATERPILLAR VALLEY, and about 300 yards to the North by N.W. of MONTAUBAN. D/162 Commanded by Captain T.St.P.Bunbury, in position under the Northern Bank of CATERPILLAR VALLEY, immediately in rear of our late 18 pounders position, due North of MONTAUBAN. The Brigade automatically became attached to 14th Divisional Arty: 33rd Division Infantry covered and supported by 14th Divisional Arty: and the two Brigades of 33rd Divisional Artillery in the line held by 33rd Division from Western edge of HIGH WOOD thence East by S.E. to a point about 500 yards N.E. of West edge of DELVILLE WOOD. 14th Division Infantry on its Right, 1st Division on its left. Front held by XV Corps in Centre with XIII on the Right and III on the left. ZONE allotted to 162nd Brigade, extreme right of 33rd Divisional Front to a point about 250 yards to the North-west. Barrage Zone, enemy extreme front line, known as WOOD LANE. All searching and sweeping of back areas done between two straight lines drawn through these two points. 14th Divisional Artillery Brigades covering the remainder of 33rd Divisional Front, 46th, 47th, 48th and 49th Brigades. Liaison Officer with Infantry Brigade (98th) found by 162nd and 166th Brigades, alternately 4 days each. Liaison Officer with Battalion H.Qrs. found by Brigades of 14th Divisional Artillery. Night firing to consist of sweeping and searching hollows and roads behind Brigade Zone. Allotment of Ammunition (expenditure of which must be maintained under all circumstances) 18 Pdrs. 415 by day. 500 by night. 4.5" How's: 233 by day. 166 by night. Per Brigade. This in addition to any Counter Battery work or minor Bombardments.	

Army Form C. 2118.

WAR DIARY
or
INTELLIGENCE SUMMARY.
(Erase heading not required.)

Instructions regarding War Diaries and Intelligence Summaries are contained in F.S. Regs., Part II. and the Staff Manual respectively. Title pages will be prepared in manuscript.

Place	Date	Hour	Summary of Events and Information	Remarks and references to Appendices
	1916. August. 12th		100th Infantry Brigade relieved by 98th Infantry Brigade. This is the following days spent in building Cover for Guns, making a thorough registration of Zone and those of Brigades covering either flank, establishing communications, O.P's and Forward O.P's. Usual day and night firing carried out in addition to registration of Zones without incident until 14th instant, when "B" & "C" Batteries area was searched and swept by 5.9's and 4.2's for about half-an-hour. The shelling was blind and resulted in only one casualty (although many had narrow escapes) consisting of One Gunner C/162 wounded and evacuated. Whole Brigade having a very much quieter time than it had from July 15th to August 1st. One Wireless set and Operator being attached to Headquarters a good many N.F. Targets were received daily, all of which (with very few exceptions) were engaged by "D" Battery.	
	15th & 16th.		Usual Day and Night Firing carried out with registration preparatory to combined attack on three Corps Front and for the Bombardment beginning on the 16th at 5 p.m. preparatory to this attack at ZERO 2.45 p.m. on the 18th. 14th and 33rd Divisional Artillery (latter consisting of 162nd and 166th Brigades) supporting 33rd Division. Objective of the latter to be WOOD LANE TRENCH from about 150 yards N.W. of its junction with ORCHARD TRENCH up to the cross roads just outside the Western corner of HIGH WOOD. XIII Corps on our Right and III Corps on our Left. The following is the gist of the preliminary bombardments and operations after various amendments to original Operation Order received at 3.30 p.m. on 16th instant.	
	16th to 18th		Between 5 p.m. and 8 a.m. on the 16th.-17th.; 17th-18th., respectively the usual Night firing was carried out with double the allotment of ammunition viz:- 18 pounders 1000 rounds., 4.5" Howitzers 332 rounds., per Brigade.	

Army Form C. 2118.

WAR DIARY
or
INTELLIGENCE SUMMARY.
(Erase heading not required.)

Instructions regarding War Diaries and Intelligence Summaries are contained in F.S. Regs., Part II. and the Staff Manual respectively. Title pages will be prepared in manuscript.

Place	Date	Hour	Summary of Events and Information	Remarks and references to Appendices
	1916. August. 16th to 18th	(Contd.)	Special attention was paid to preventing the enemy repairing damage or re-inforcing. Howitzers on Road-junctions and points in rear; 18 pounders and on front line and searching and sweeping hollows and approaches in rear. Day Bombardments of 17th was continuous 18 pounders bombarding WOOD LANE at intervals, cutting wire and searching the ground between the right and left of our Zone as far as SWITCH TRENCH. The Ground between our own and the enemy Trenches was searched at intervals, our own Front Trenches being cleared for the purpose. On August 18th Bombardment resumed at 6 a.m. on the same Targets as on the 17th except (1) There were two intervals during which the Howitzers lifted on to SWITCH TRENCH. 1st interval 8 a.m. to 8.40 a.m. 2nd interval 11.10 a.m. to 12.10 p.m. (2) Intense Bombardment by all 18 pounders from 8.40 a.m. to 8.47. a.m. and from 12.10 p.m. to 12.19 p.m. Guns were concentrated on the Front Line and fired at the rate of 3 rounds per Gun per minute. Howitzers dropped back on the Front Line Trenches at 8.45 a.m. and 12.15 p.m. During the intervals 8 to 8.40 a.m. and 11.10 a.m. to 12.10 p.m. the fire of 18 pounders was intermittent and not heavy, being sufficient merely to prevent movement in the Trenches and to search Ground behind the Hostile Trenches and between our own and the Hostile Trenches. There was no firing before the five minutes intense Bombardment. At 1.45 p.m. the Howitzers ceased firing 18 pounders continued intermittently, but the ground between the opposing trenches was searched for the first 10 minutes only. In order to make the start of the Infantry from our Trenches simultaneous along the whole front of our attacking front, there was no intense bombardment before ZERO. An intense bombardment by 18 pounders on the Trenches to be assaulted started at ZERO. At ZERO the Infantry were ordered to keep up as close as possible under our Barrage and to assault their objectives immediately the barrage lifted off the latter.	

Army Form C. 2118.

WAR DIARY
or
INTELLIGENCE SUMMARY.
(Erase heading not required.)

Instructions regarding War Diaries and Intelligence Summaries are contained in F. S. Regs., Part II. and the Staff Manual respectively. Title pages will be prepared in manuscript.

Place	Date	Hour	Summary of Events and Information	Remarks and references to Appendices.
	1916. August. 16/18.		At 5 minutes after ZERO 18 pounders searched back quickly by lifts of 50 yards, 1 round per Gun each lift for 200 yards and kept up a barrage on that line for 10 minutes, at 2 rounds per Gun per min: At ZERO 4.5" Howitzers turned on SWITCH TRENCH which they bombarded for one hour and at frequent intervals during the following two hours. At 15 minutes after ZERO all 18 pounders searched back another 200 yards, (viz:- 400 yards in rear of German Front Line). At 17 minutes after ZERO half the 18 pounders (alternate sections from the right) searched the ground, trenches and approaches further back, the remaining section forming a close barrage 400 yards beyond the enemy's present front line trenches, by sweeping at the rate of 1½ rounds per Gun per minute. The Net result of the Operations were as follows:- Objectives gained on III and XIII and right of XV Corps front 33rd Division again driven back to original line, by flanking Machine Gun fire and Machine Gun fire from Shell holes in front of Objectives. At about half-an-hour after ZERO when this was realized our Brigade shortened its barrage to a point 200 yards N.E. of WOOD LANE and continued a barrage on that line until Orders were received from Headqrs: 14th Div: Arty: to lift another 100 yards as situation of 14th Division on our right still obscure and it was feared our barrage might catch their Infantry. Situation report received soon afterwards entirely justified the shortening of our Barrage.	
	19th		At about 7.30 p.m. the Brigade returned to its normal night firing. Received Orders at about 7 p.m. to side-slip our Zone about 200 yards to the right. Normal day and night firing. Registered New Zone and carried out usual day and night firing.	
	20th		Recived Orders for new attack, to take last line of enemy Trench inside DELVILLE WOOD by the 14th Division on our right in which we were to co-operate in taking a part of WOOD LANE on 33rd Division's right on 21st.	

Army Form C. 2118.

WAR DIARY
or
INTELLIGENCE SUMMARY.
(Erase heading not required.)

Instructions regarding War Diaries and Intelligence Summaries are contained in F. S. Regs., Part II. and the Staff Manual respectively. Title pages will be prepared in manuscript.

Place	Date	Hour	Summary of Events and Information	Remarks and references to Appendices.
	1916. August. 21st.		Short preliminary bombardment at 3.30 p.m. carried out, but enterprise unsuccessful. At about 3 p.m. received orders to reconnoitre position for single Gun to enfilade New German Trench running about N.E. from WOOD LANE and running into the latter. Reange to be not less than 2000 yards from the N.E. edge of Trench. O.C., Brigade took bearings on trench from O.P. and thence reconnoitred position, which he finally chose on Southern edge of road running W. and E. due North of BAZENTIN-LE-GRANDE. Gun to be place in a shell hole. Range to S.W. edge of Trench 1600 yards.	
		7 p.m.	Orders received for a further attack on part of Right Brigade of 33rd Division. This time objective to be a part of TEA TRENCH running in a N.E. direction from its Junction with WOOD LANE. ZERO hour to be 1.30 a.m. Infantry again unsuccessful, finding the Trench very strongly held both with Men and Machine Guns. Heavy casualties incurred from Machine Gun fire and shelling. Usual night firing resumed at about 2.30 a.m. 22nd.	
	22nd.		Usual day firing carried out without incident. At about 4 p.m. definite Orders received to establish one 18 pdr. in enfilade position North of BAZENTIN-LE-GRANDE and to register the following day. 300 rounds.,(chiefly shrapnel.) to be kept up with Gun.Lieut.V. BENNETT STANFORD C/162 put in Command of Gun which was put into position and registered with 70 rounds on 23rd instant, a large majority of which burst immediately over and into the enemy Trench at true enfilade.	
	23rd		Orders received at about 7 p.m. for a renewal of the attack on 24th instant. This to be the biggest 'push' since the 13th and 14th July. French attacking simultaneously with FOURTH ARMY from the SOMME TO MAUREPAS, XV Corps to attack from the South of GUILLEMONT - South West edge of GINCHY Village.	

Army Form C. 2118.

WAR DIARY
or
INTELLIGENCE SUMMARY.
(Erase heading not required.)

Place	Date	Hour	Summary of Events and Information	Remarks and references to Appendices
	1916. August. 23rd.		14th Division to advance right of their line so as to connect up with left of XIV Corps; to clear remainder of DELVILLE WOOD; to establish a line outside DELVILLE WOOD from position already held by the Division in BEER TRENCH to LONGUEVAL-FLERS Road and to connect there with 33rd Division. The III Corps to attack part of the intermediate line, Thus, Order of Battle in the attack from right to left:- French from SOMME to MAUREPAS. XIV Corps from South of GUILLEMONT to Western Edge of GINCHY village. XV Corps. from point in LONGUEVAL-FLERS Road N. of DELVILLE WOOD to Western edge of HIGH WOOD. III Corps.from Western edge of HIGH WOOD to extreme left of attack Task of this Brigade:- To support the left Battalion 'QUEENS' of the Right Brigade (100th Infantry Brigade) in WOOD LANE. ZERO hour to be at 5.45 p.m. on 24th. Bombardment to begin at 3.45 p.m. From 3.45 p.m. to 5.50 p.m. our Batteries bombarded NEW TRENCH behind WOOD LANE and ground and communications in rear at a rate of 1 round per gun per 2 minutes, and TEA TRENCH, TEA LANE, and TEA SUPPORT, (West of LONGUEVAL-FLERS Road) but cheifly on TEA TRENCH at rate of one round per gun per minute. From 5.45 p.m. to 6.50 p.m. Enfilade Gun North of BAZENTIN-LE-GRANDE, on NEW TRENCH about one round per minute, last 10 minutes 2 rounds per minute. This gun was ordered to retain 150 rounds and be ready in the event of a Counter attack. At 6.45 p.m. at which time the Infantry were to take NEW TRENCH the Gun was to switch on the left and to cease fire at 6.50 p.m. From 5.50 p.m. to 6.45 p.m. 18 pounders to continue as before 1½ rounds per Gun per minute - same target and rate of Fire for Hows: At 6.45 p.m. our 18 pounders to continue and open an intense shrapnel fire at 4 rounds per gun per minute. Howitzers (D/162) to lift to FLERS-LONGUEVAL Road at rate of 1 Round per How: per 2 minutes, until 6.50 p.m. when the 18 pounders searched back for 25 yards every 4½ minutes at 3 rounds minute. Afterwards with no cessation of	

Army Form C. 2118.

WAR DIARY
or
INTELLIGENCE SUMMARY.
(Erase heading not required.)

Instructions regarding War Diaries and Intelligence Summaries are contained in F. S. Regs., Part II. and the Staff Manual respectively. Title pages will be prepared in manuscript.

Place	Date	Hour	Summary of Events and Information	Remarks and references to Appendices
	1916. August. 23rd. (Contd)		cessation of firing until they arrived at a line about 200 yards N.E. of where our Infantry would be. A sweeping fire to be kept up at a rate of 4 rounds per Gun per minute until 7.5.p.m. when alternate sections of 18 pounders searched the ground behind the remainder continuing a close barrage by sweeping. The Rate of fire to be two rounds per Gun per minute for the first 10 minutes, afterwards dropping to one round per Gun per minute. From 6.50 p.m. until 8.45p.m. the Howitzer Fire was to become intermittent and gradually to die down, not ceasing however before daylight. From 7.45 p.m to 8.45 p.m the rates of fire of 18-pdrs were to be halved if the situation permitted when they would cease a close barrage, but continue to search ground behind and all approaches & trenches within range at frequent intervals throughout the night, all batteries remaining particularly alert for an S.O.S. signal.	
	24th		Orders as above carried out with most satisfactory results. All objectives gained on XV Corps front with the exception that the easternmost corner of DELVILLE WOOD was not quite cleared and only a part of BEER TRENCH was taken. Of the 3 battalions of 98th Brigade K.R.R's and WORCESTERS suffered very few casualties but the QUEENS were badly shelled and lost a good many Officers and men. The French were extremely successful at MAUREPAS but III Corps were not sosuccessful and failed to take the intermediate line. During the night up to 1030 p.m we continued a close barrage of one round per gun per minute after which we slowed down to a steady barrage of 2 rounds per minute with an occasional burst of fire on the enemy front line in order to give the Infantry the opportunity of consolidating the ground gained. This fire was kept up until 7.30a.m 25th.	
	25th		33rd Division and General LAIRD in particular congratulated on the great success of the enterprise. Total number of prisoners taken by XV Corps was 9 Officers 189 O.R. General SANDYS, G.O.C., R.A.,	

Army Form C. 2118.

WAR DIARY
or
INTELLIGENCE SUMMARY.
(Erase heading not required.)

Place	Date	Hour	Summary of Events and Information	Remarks and references to Appendices
4th Division	August 25th 1916 (Contd)		XIV Corps sent special congratulations to 162nd Brigade R.F.A. for the splendid support given the infantry by all ranks and congratulated the O.C. Brigade personally for the promptness of his reports on the situation from the O.P. which he said he was able to pass on to 33rd Divisional Headquarters direct, the information reaching the G.O.C. before it had been received from any other source and thus proving of the greatest value. The enfilade gun particularly did great service and many dead were found in the enemy trench thus again proving the enormous value of true enfilade fire. There was however one very disappointing feature of the operations viz: the appalling number of "duds" amongst the shells of our heavy artillery – in all there must have been 60% which either did not detonate at all or gave only a small explosion instead of a real detonation. As regards this highly important feature of an attack the unsatisfactory quality of our heavy shells or fuze was particularly emphasised by contrast with the German Heavy Artillery. The Ammunition he is employing on this Front cannot give a greater percentage of "Blinds" than 5% at the maximum, and the damage done by the detonations of his heavy shells – and in particular his 150 mm. – is appalling. At 8 a.m. the enemy gave the first symptoms of angry retaliation, for our successes of the previous day and unfortunately for the Brigade he chose our 18 pounder Batteries upon which to wreak his first vengeance, for nearly 36 hours he rained the Guns Positions at intervals with 8"., 150 mm., and 105 mm., and made it quite impossible for the Men to remain at the Guns. Fortunately a good trench runs in rear of the positions and Battery Commanders ordered every man to take cover in this Trench. At about 8.30 a.m. Major R.G.M.Johnston, (Commanding "B"/162) was killed by a piece of shell which hit him in the side. His Battery had left cover during the a temporary lull of the shelling, and he himself was getting his ammunition wagons away after unloading, when the shelling opened again. He at once ordered every one to the Trench again but unfortunately was the last to take cover himself and was hit just as he reached the Trench.	

Army Form C. 2118.

WAR DIARY
or
INTELLIGENCE SUMMARY.
(Erase heading not required.)

Instructions regarding War Diaries and Intelligence Summaries are contained in F.S. Regs., Part II. and the Staff Manual respectively. Title pages will be prepared in manuscript.

Place	Date	Hour	Summary of Events and Information	Remarks and references to Appendices
	1916. August. 25th (Contd).		The Brigade could ill-spare him, and he has left a blank which it is impossible to fill. The total number of casualties in the two days during which this shelling lasted reached 3 Officers and 3 Other ranks, of the 3 Officers, 2nd Lieut.E.M.I.Body, "B"/162, was wounded in the leg, but was able to remain at duty. 2nd Lieut.G.H.A. Huddart, A/162, was badly wounded in the head, and evacuated. Of the 3 Other ranks, all were of "B" Battery, two of whom were killed, including their Signalling Corporal, a Man who had done invaluable service to the Battery. Positions so obliterated by Shell Fire that new Positions had to be taken up. One Gun completely destroyed. O.C., Brigade reconnoitred New Positions and finally decided upon Slope about 500 yards N.E. of Late positions. This move was partially effected the same night and completed the next day. In the evening notice from 14th Divisional Artillery was received to the effect that our zone would be changed the following day, and positions were to be taken up within 4000 yards of New Zone. Fortunately our New positions met the requirements and registration was duly begun on the next day.	
	26th		Our New Zones to be immediately N.E. of DELVILLE WOOD, a side-slip to the Right of about 800 yards. 47th and 46th Brigades R.F.A. on our immediate Right and Left respectively. Fortunately our Present O.P(s were suitable, after a good registration had been carried out. This was done during the day. Original Zones still to be covered until further Orders, and usual Day and Night firing carried out.	
	27th		Orders received at 3.10 p.m. to assume New Zones. These were taken over at 3.15 p.m. and the usual Day and Night firing was carried out. Brigade Liaison Officer duties allotted to the Brigade, the other Brigades going Battalions. We covered the left Battalion of Right Brigade of 14th Division., viz., KYO.Y.L.I. This Battalion and that on their Right made exceptionally good progress during the 26th and 27th	

Army Form C. 2118.

WAR DIARY
or
INTELLIGENCE SUMMARY.
(Erase heading not required.)

Place	Date	Hour	Summary of Events and Information	Remarks and references to Appendices
	1916. August. 27th. (Contd).		and 27th. taking a portion of BEER TRENCH and clearing the remaining parts of DELVILLE WOOD held by the enemy. This was done with only minor support by Artillery and chiefly by Bombing attacks. In all, during this period they took about 80 prisoners.	
	28/29th.		Usual Day and Night firing carried out, and registration checked. Guns dug in and camouflaged, and recesses dug for ammunition. Re-newal of attack by FOURTH ARMY and the FRENCH originally meant to take place on 29th and 30th, but post-poned owing to the bad weather conditions.	
	30th. & 31st.		33rd and 14th Divisions (less R.A.) relieved by 24th Division. Weather of the very worst. Much rain and wind. Heavy shelling of the VALLEY and many of the Battery Positions during the 30th and 31st. Our Batteries fortunately escaped lightly. On the 31st afternoon at about 1 p.m. Germans attacked the whole line from HIGH-WOOD to E. and S.E. of DELVILLE WOOD. Fortunately Captain A.B.Van STRAUBENZEE, and 2nd Lieut. M.M.I.Body, at the O.P's got a firm grasp of the situation and got all the 18 pounders of the Brigade on to a large body of the enemy which was advancing in COCOA LANE. On our own front the Infantry held their ground, but for some time the general situation was obscure. Ultimately it was found that the part of TEA TRENCH N. of FLERS Road and a part of WOOD LANE had been evacuated by our Infantry who reported that they were shelled out by Heavy Artillery Fire.	

Army Form C. 2118.

WAR DIARY
or
INTELLIGENCE SUMMARY.
(Erase heading not required.)

Place	Date	Hour	Summary of Events and Information	Remarks and references to Appendices
	1916. August.		CASUALTIES:	
			Officers:- Killed.	
			Major R.G.M.Johnston 25th.	
			Wounded and evacuated.	
			2nd Lieut.J.C.M.Filgate. 23rd.	
			2nd Lieut.G.H.A.Huddart. 25th.	
			Wounded and remaind at Duty.	
			2nd Lieut.M.M.I.Body. 25th.	
			Posted. Lieut.B.R.Heape. 7th.	
			2nd Lieut.B.S.M.Paterson. 2nd.	
			2nd Lieut.V.H.Westerby. 8th.	
			2nd Lieut.R.C.Odnams. 25th.	
			Other Ranks.	
			KILLED. 3. Joined........ 61.	
			Died of wounds. 1. Posted away...... 6.	
			Wounded & evactd. 9.	
			Wounded (at duty) 6.	

Lieut.Colonel.R.F.A.
Commanding 162nd Brigade. R.F.A.

Army Form C. 2118.

82 vol 10 162nd Brigade TFA

WAR DIARY
or
INTELLIGENCE SUMMARY
(Erase heading not required.)

Instructions regarding War Diaries and Intelligence Summaries are contained in F.S. Regs., Part II. and the Staff Manual respectively. Title Pages will be prepared in manuscript.

Place	Date 1916.	Hour	Summary of Events and Information	Remarks and references to Appendices
	September, 1st.		Usual Day and Night firing carried out. Orders received that postponed attack of FRENCH and FOURTH ARMY would take place on 3rd instant, to be preceded by preliminary bombardment on 2nd and 3rd instants. Memo: received from 33rd Divisional Artillery stating that Military Medals had been awarded on 30th August to- No.13112 Corporal G.H.Vinter, Headquarterstaff. No.52723 A/Bombr. C.R.Newnes, "A" Battery. No.83204 Corporal S.J.Tooth, "B" Battery. No.36015 Corporal A.J.Whale, "C" Battery. These were awarded for excellent work on communications and bravery and perseverance under heavy shell fire. Act/Bombr. C.R.Newnes was with 2nd Lieut.V.Hailey, when the later was wounded, and under heavy fire fetched up a stretcher to take him away. Unfortunately Corporal Tooth was killed 5 days before he was awarded the Medal.	
	2nd		Bombardment in connection with attack on the 3rde commenced at 8 a.m. The French attacked simultaneously with the Fourth Army. Order of Battle in the attack - French on the Right. Fourth Army on the Left from GUILLEMONT to extreme left of attack which joined the right of the Reserve Army in front of THIEPVAL. Fourth Army composed of- Right XIV Corps. Centre XV Corps. Left III Corps. XIV Corps attacked FALFEMONT FARM and GUILLEMONT, and was ordered to establish itself on a line of road from WEDGE WOOD to GINCHY, as far North as right of XV Corps front.	

Army Form C. 2118.

WAR DIARY
or
INTELLIGENCE SUMMARY

(Erase heading not required.)

Instructions regarding War Diaries and Intelligence Summaries are contained in F. S. Regs., Part II. and the Staff Manual respectively. Title Pages will be prepared in manuscript.

Place	Date	Hour	Summary of Events and Information	Remarks and references to Appendices
	September, 1916. 2nd (Contd.)		XV Corps attacked Village of GINCHY and Trenches round it 300 yards to its South including the Trench east of the Village VAT ALLEY, PINT TRENCH, to its Junction with ALE ALLEY and ALE ALLEY. 24th Division Ordered to capture BEER TRENCH from its Junction with ALE ALLEY, or such portions of this Trench as had not been previously captured. To re-take that part of WOOD LANE which they had lost during the two previous days, and to link up with the 1st Division on their left. 1st Division Ordered to attack N.E. half of WOOD LANE and the German intermediate line, both in HIGH WOOD and 2000 yards west of HIGH WOOD. The task of the 162nd Brigade. R.F.A. was to support Left Battalion of the 72nd Infantry Brigade, being the right Brigade of the 24th Division. Special injunctions were issued by Commander-in-chief stating that these operations were of the utmost importance, and desiring it to be impressed on all Officers to satisfy themselves thoroughly that all under their Command fully understood what was required of them, that all plans and preparations should be complete and thorough, and that no detail should be overlooked and no possible aid to success unemployed. During the whole of to-day the bombardment continued and throughout, the night on our specially allotted Targets. By dint of constant nursing and care on the part of the Battery Commanders the Guns and Howitzers stood the test very well, and by ZERO hours all 12 18 pounders and 4 4.5" Howitzers were intact.	

Army Form C. 2118.

WAR DIARY
or
INTELLIGENCE SUMMARY

(Erase heading not required.)

Instructions regarding War Diaries and Intelligence Summaries are contained in F. S. Regs., Part II. and the Staff Manual respectively. Title Pages will be prepared in manuscript.

Place	Date	Hour	Summary of Events and Information	Remarks and references to Appendices
	September, 1916. 3rd.		ZERO hour 12 noon. O.C., Brigade observed from his own and Battery O.P's in the Old German Second Line, West of DELVILLE WOOD where an excellent view of the attack could be obtained from HIGH WOOD to N.E. of DELVILLE WOOD. At 12.15 p.m. the Cameron Highlanders of 1st Division were seen to advance into WOOD LANE, practically without opposition. Parties proceeded round the Eastern corner and along the N.E. face of the Trench. Towards the East they reached a point 50 yards in front of the enemy trench. Parties were also seen to cross WOOD LANE and to jump into the trench running eastward along the Crest. At 12.30 p.m. a Second Infantry Regiment was seen to leave BLACK WATCH TRENCH (about 300 yards in rear of WOOD LANE) and advance towards the latter under Heavy Machine Gun fire from the sky their right front. The Camerons were still seen to be advancing over the line to the East of HIGH WOOD and seemed to be working towards NEW TRENCH which runs at its right angle to WOOD LANE. At 1.25 p.m. a Party of the enemy appeared to be holding them up, but the Camerons surrounded them to the North and bombing encounters took place. Our Infantry, however, were able to advance further down WOOD LANE. The whole of the remainder of the Camerons had disappeared over the sky line towards SWITCH TRENCH where it appears they were stopped and suffered severe casualties. No movement was seen from the left of 24th Division. During the whole of this period there was very little Hostile Fire except for a medium 5.9" barrage on DELVILLE WOOD.	

Army Form C. 2118.

WAR DIARY
or
INTELLIGENCE SUMMARY

(Erase heading not required.)

Instructions regarding War Diaries and Intelligence Summaries are contained in F. S. Regs., Part II. and the Staff Manual respectively. Title Pages will be prepared in manuscript.

Place	Date	Hour	Summary of Events and Information	Remarks and references to Appendices
	September, 1916. 3rd (contd).		Meanwhile everything had gone well on our own Brigade Zone where very little had to be done, the attacking being all on either flank, although the bombardment was of the same nature on this front as on others. At 2 p.m. on Report from 14th Divisional Artillery that large numbers of the enemy were collecting in SWITCH TRENCH for 200 yards East of FLERS-LONGUEVAL Road. D/162 fired Gun fire for 15 minutes on this point after which a slow rate was kept up on this Target until 4 p.m. At about 3.25 p.m. Germans were seen to advance Eastwards on WOOD LANE, our Infantry retiring about 200 yards in front of them. The Germans came from a N.E'ly direction, entered the Eastern corner of HIGH WOOD; the N.W. portion of WOOD LANE and Trench running east along the crest. We still held the southern portion of WOOD LANE. 9 Guns of our Brigade were pulled out of the Pits and switched over on to the enemy counter attack. The Germans did not advance more than 30 yards over the Crest, but remain in their Trench along the Crest line as seen from S.16 b. Small parties of Boches could be seen advancing west from the Gate that stands out on the sky line about midway between HIGH and DELVILLE Woods. At 3.35 p.m. the enemy were occupying the whole of the skyline from HIGH WOOD 500 yards Eastwards. They appeared to be unmolested by any other Artillery Fire than our own. There was certainly a barrage of sorts but it was well over the Crest and was late in starting. At about 5.50 p.m. small parties of our troops were seen retiring from the direction of SWITCH TRENCH, actually from WOOD LANE Eastwards. Between 50 to 100 were seen to return.	

Army Form C. 2118.

WAR DIARY
or
INTELLIGENCE SUMMARY
(Erase heading not required.)

162nd Brigade R.F.A., SEPTEMBER 1916.

Instructions regarding War Diaries and Intelligence Summaries are contained in F.S. Regs., Part II. and the Staff Manual respectively. Title Pages will be prepared in manuscript.

Place	Date	Hour	Summary of Events and Information	Remarks and references to Appendices
	1916 September 3rd (contd).		Thus on this front the whole attack was rendered utterly fruitless by the troops apparently being ignorant of the nature and locality of their objectives and consequently finding little resistance overan the points to be taken and were cut up in retiring. The final result was that our line at 7 p.m between HIGH & DELVILLE WOODS was the same as before the attack and the sacrifice had been appalling. The attack itself in its initial stages was as fine as there has ever been and had the promises of a great victory. On the rest of the front **great** successes were met. GINCHY was taken, lost, and re-taken on the following day. GUILLEMONT was taken and the French were successful along the whole of the front taking 3000 Prisoners and 12 guns.	
	September 4th		Usual day and night firing carried out. In the afternoon we co-operated in another effort to clear east corner of DELVILLE WOOD and ALE & HOP ALLEYS which had not been entirely taken the previous day. 4 Battery Commanders came to get into touch with the front, the 2nd N.Z. Bde being ordered to relieve us on 5-6th. More successes by the French who took 12 Kilometres more trenches and 1700 Prisoners.	
	September 5th		One Section per Battery of 2nd N.Z.Bde came up and took over from our batteries and registered their guns. Usual day and night firing carried out. News received of further successes of the French who reached BAPAUME-PERONNE Road, took CHILLY, BARLEUX. many prisoners, 17 guns and one Kite Balloon. XIV Corps took LEUZE AND BOULEAUX WOODS.	
	September 6th		Remaining Sections of N.Z.Bde took over from us and we proceeded to BONNAY(via our wagon lines at BECORDEL), where the whole Bde arrived during the evening.	

Army Form C. 2118.

WAR DIARY
INTELLIGENCE SUMMARY

(Erase heading not required.)

162nd Brigade R.F.A., SEPTEMBER 1916.

Instructions regarding War Diaries and Intelligence Summaries are contained in F.S. Regs., Part II. and the Staff Manual respectively. Title Pages will be prepared in manuscript.

Place	Date	Hour	Summary of Events and Information	Remarks and references to Appendices
	1916 September 7th		Brigade left BONNAY about 9.30 a.m & arrived at WARGNIES about 6 p.m	
	8th		Brigade left WARGNIES about 9 a.m and arrived at LE MEILLARD about 1 p.m	
	9th		Brigade left LE MEILLARD about 9.30 a.m and arrived at LUCHEUX about 2.30 p.m	
	10th		Brigade Left LUCHEUX about 7 a.m and arrived at WANQUENTIN about 10.30 a.m where wagon lines were established.	
	13th		Orders received to relieve the 123rd Brigade R.F.A. 37th Div. Arty. A Section of each Battery marched to positions near DAINVILLE during the evening and went into action there.	
	14th		Remainder of batteries and Brigade H.Q., marched. Brigade H.Q., took over "C" Group from 123rd Brigade H.Q., and were situated in a white house on the main ARRAS-DOULLENS Road just south of the church in DAINVILLE. The Group was composed of our own batteries and "C"/63 & "D"/64 of 12th Div. Arty. We were under 12th Div. Arty for fighting, 33rd Div. Arty acting as "Q" at ROSSEUX CHATEAU. It was a distance of 9 kilometres from wagon lines to Bde H.Q.,	
	15th		Orders received late in the evening that we were to move straightway to VII Corps area. ("These orders stopped leave which had been re-opened the same day at the rate of 3 per Brigade every Wednesday. 7 vacancies had been allotted to the Bde for men to go to the rest camp at BOULOGNE, but these were also cancelled.). Bde H.Q., and one Section from each battery	

Army Form C. 2118.

162nd Brigade R.F.A.,   SEPTEMBER 1916   WAR DIARY or INTELLIGENCE SUMMARY

(Erase heading not required.)

Instructions regarding War Diaries and Intelligence Summaries are contained in F. S. Regs., Part II. and the Staff Manual respectively. Title Pages will be prepared in manuscript.

Place	Date 1916	Hour	Summary of Events and Information	Remarks and references to Appendices
	September 15th (contd) 16th		moved to wagon lines at WANQUENTIN immediately. Remainder of Brigade moved out evening of 16th. Positions were left vacant. Bde H.Q., and one Section from each Battery left WANQUENTIN about 9 a.m and marched to PAS where wagon lines were established near PAS HUTS just outside the village. The 4 Battery Sections moved into action straightaway on the GOMMECOURT FRONT, relieving respective Sections of batteries of the 81st Brigade R.F.A. 17th Division. Bde H.Q., left PAS in the afternoon and marched to SOUASTRE where headquarters were opened at No.4, where they remained until 20th.	
	17th		Remainder of Brigade moved into action night of 17/18th. Brigade under orders of 17th Div. Arty for fighting.	
	19th		162nd Bde H.Q., took over from 81st Bde H.Q., and commanded the "Centre Group" 17th Div. Arty (consisting only of our own batteries.	
	20th		One Section of each Battery relieved one Section of each of the batteries of the 73th Brigade R.F.A., forming the NORTHERN GROUP, 17th Div. Arty., and 162nd Bde H.Q., took over command of "Northern Group" from 73th Brigade H.Q., The remainder of the Brigade were to relieve the remainder of the 73th Brigade R.F.A. on the night 21st, but this was cancelled late in the evening. One Section per Battery was left in action and the remainder moved to wagon lines at PAS the same night. The relieving Div. Arty was the 46th.	
	22nd		Remaining The respective sections of batteries still in action moved to wagon line on night 22/23. Brigade Headquarters moved direct to WANQUENTIN, where wagon lines were again established.	

2449 Wt. W14957/Mgo 750,000 1/16 J.B.C. & A. Forms/C.2118/12.

Army Form C. 2118.

WAR DIARY
INTELLIGENCE SUMMARY
(Erase heading not required.)

162nd Brigade R.F.A., SEPTEMBER 1916.

Instructions regarding War Diaries and Intelligence Summaries are contained in F. S. Regs., Part II. and the Staff Manual respectively. Title Pages will be prepared in manuscript.

Place	Date	Hour	Summary of Events and Information	Remarks and references to Appendices
	1916 September 2nd		2 Sections per battery went into action near DAINVILLE. They came under the command of Colonel HEXT 12th Div. Arty "G" Group. Our own headquarters remained in WANQUENTIN.	
	23rd		Remaining Section per Battery went into action.	
			----------o0o----------	
			A D D E N D A.	
			Divisional Artilleries re-organised. 162nd Brigade's composition altered as follows:-	
			OLD FORMATION. NEW FORMATION.	
			½ "A"/162 plus "C"/167 "A"/162 (6-18 pdr guns).	
			½ "A"/162 plus "B"/162 "B"/162 (6-18 pdr guns).	
			½ "B"/167 plus "C"/162 "C"/162 (6-18 pdr guns).	
	with 12th effect from 12 noon.		"D"/162 remains "D"/162 (4-4.5" Howitzers)	
			----------o0o----------	

2449 Wt. W14957/M90 750,000 1/16 J.B.C. & A. Forms/C.2118/12.

Army Form C. 2118.

WAR DIARY
~~INTELLIGENCE SUMMARY~~
(Erase heading not required.)

162nd Brigade R.F.A., SEPTEMBER 1916.

Place	Date	Hour	Summary of Events and Information	Remarks and references to Appendices
			C A S U A L T I E S .	

OFFICERS.
Sick - Capt F.C.Packham (To 33rd D.A.C., 12th).
Joined - Capt.G.Fetherston, ⎫
2nd Lieut A.R.Tucker.   ⎬ From Old "C"/167.
2nd Lieut J.R.B.Turner.   ⎭
2nd Lieut E.J.G.Chapman. } Now "A"/162.
2nd Lieut J.H.K.Rayson, ⎫
2nd Lieut J.R.Barnes.   ⎬ From Old "B"/167.(Now "C"/162)
2nd Lieut D.Fitch.   ⎭
Major J.D.Belgrave, D.S.O., from 2nd Division to Command "D"/162.

Posted AWAY.- Lieut H.C.Cory to "B"/162 from Old 167th Bde H.Q.,
2nd Lieut L.M.Howard to 33rd D.A.C.,

MEN.
Sick - 22 (all evacuated).
Wounded - one on 1-9-1916.
          one on 17-9-16.
          one on 18-9-16.

Joined - 237 (including those posted from Old "C"/167 & "B"/167
Posted away to other units - 17.

HORSES.
Posted away - 40. (Evacuated to M.V.S).
Joined - 180 (including those posted from old "C"/167 & "B"/167
Deaths - 2.

F.T.O.

Army Form C. 2118.

WAR DIARY
or
INTELLIGENCE SUMMARY
(Erase heading not required.)

162nd Brigade R.F.A., SEPTEMBER 1916.

Place	Date	Hour	Summary of Events and Information	Remarks and references to Appendices

H O N O U R S.

During the month the undermentioned awards were made to the following for acts of gallantry in the Field. (SOMME).

Capt. G.Fetherston }
Lieut. V.Benett Stanford } - MILITARY CROSS.
Capt. A.B.Van Straubenzee }

13112 Corpl. G.H.Vinter }
83204 Corpl. S.J.Tooth } - MILITARY MEDAL.
32723 A/Bombdr.C.R.Newnes }
36015 Corpl A.J.Withal }

W.H. Reid
Lieut-Col R.F.A.,
Commanding 162nd Brigade R.F.A.

162nd BRIGADE R.F.A., WAR DIARY Army Form C. 2118.
INTELLIGENCE SUMMARY OCTOBER 1916.

(Erase heading not required.)

Instructions regarding War Diaries and Intelligence Summaries are contained in F.S. Regs, Part II. and the Staff Manual respectively. Title Pages will be prepared in manuscript.

162 2 Bde R.F.A. Vol II

Place	Date	Hour	Summary of Events and Information	Remarks and references to Appendices
	3rd		One Section per Battery came out of action on the ARRAS front and marched to wagon lines at WANQUETIN.	
	4th		These Sections and Brigade Headquarters marched from WANQUETIN to GAUDIEMPRE where new wagon lines were established in VII Corps area Third Army. The Sections went into action on GOMMECOURT front, covering 49th Divisional Infantry, in the following positions :- (Ref: Map 57 D.N.E., 1/20,000). "A" Battery. K.2.a.30.67.) These positions "B" Battery. K.2.a.50.66.) just south of "C" Battery. K.2.d.04.63.) FONQUEVILLERS. "D" Battery. J.6.b.7.5. (Near Chateau de la Haie). Headquarters J.6.d.3.9. (Near Chateau de la Haie).	The Batteries were in a position from which they could barrage the hostile trenches west of GOMMECOURT by enfilade fire and could also cut wire on the various hostile lines east of HEBUTERNE as far as ROSSIGNOL WOOD.
	5th & 6th 6th & 7th		2nd Section marched as per 1st Section. 3rd Section per 18-pdr battery marched as per 1st Section.	
	8th		"D"/162 exchanged positions with a How: Battery of 48th Div'l Arty. from J.6.b.7.5 to K.9.c.3.7. (in HEBUTERNE). 1 gun of "B"/162 removed to E.26.d.6.5 (in FONQUEVILLERS) to do wire cutting on front at E.28.c.6.4.	
	12th		33rd Divisional Infantry (19th Infantry Brigade) relieved 49th Divisional Infantry.	
	17th & 18th		Brigade Commander reconnoitred positions for Batteries on the SERRE front.	

To sheet 2.

Army Form C. 2118.

WAR DIARY
~~INTELLIGENCE SUMMARY~~

162nd BRIGADE R.F.A., OCTOBER 1916.
Sheet 2.

(*Erase heading not required.*)

Place	Date	Hour	Summary of Events and Information	Remarks and references to Appendices
	19th & 20th		Batteries and Headquarters moved into XIII Corps area, Reserve Army and took up new positions as follows:— Headquarters J.18.c.8.8. (In SAILLY-AU-BOIS). Ref: Map "A" Battery K.23.c.1.7.) 57 D.N.E. "B" Battery K.21.c.25.95.) SOUTH of HEBUTERNE. 1/20,000 "C" Battery K.21.a.5.3.) "D" Battery K.15.b.85.10. (In HEBUTERNE). The Brigade now formed Corps Artillery and was responsible for cutting wire on a front from K.23.d.90.65 to K.23.b.57.30, the line on our front being held by 31st Division. This front extended west of PUISIEUX and as far south as SERRE.	
	20th		Wagon Lines moved from GAUDIEMPRE to ST. LEGER LES AUTHIE. I.12.b.5.2. (Ref: Map 57d. 1/40,000).	
	21st		Registering new Zone.	
	22-31st		Destruction of the wire on Brigade front to clear a passage for Infantry assault. Night firing to keep open and prevent repairs on gaps made in wire, Enemy approaches, communication trenches, and trench junctions.	
	26th		Raid made by 93rd Infantry Brigade. 2 Artillery bombardments – 7.30 p.m to 8.0 p.m & 10.0 p.m to 10.40 p.m. The state of NO MAN'S LAND caused raiding party to withdraw to our own trenches without having penetrated those of the enemy.	
	29th		18-pdr batteries were rather heavily shelled during the day, A disused gun pit doing duty as a signallers' dug-out received a direct hit from a 4" H.V. Shell causing 9 casualties – 5 Killed and 4 wounded. (One of the Killed being the Wireless Operator attached from R.F.C).	

Army Form C. 2118.

WAR DIARY
& INTELLIGENCE SUMMARY
(Erase heading not required.)

162nd BRIGADE R.F.A.,

OCTOBER 1916

Sheet 3.

Place	Date	Hour	Summary of Events and Information	Remarks and references to Appendices
			OCTOBER CASUALTIES.	
			OFFICERS.	
			2nd Lieut T.R.Mayler posted to "V"/33 Heavy T.M.Battery. 8-10-16.	
			Lieut & Adjt. T.D.Shepherd wounded in action 14-10-16.	
			2nd Lieut M.M.I.Body wounded in action 19-10-16.	
			MEN.	
			Killed - 6 (including 2 attached).	
			Wounded and Evacuated - 10.	
			Wounded and remained at duty - 3.	
			Sick :- Admitted to Hospital - 41.	
			Evacuated - 29.	
			Discharged to duty - 12.	
			Joined as Reinforcements - 48.	
			Posted away to other units - 1.	
			HORSES.	
			Posted away - 25 (To M.V.S., & evacuated).	
			Joined - 33	
			Deaths - 1 Killed.	
	2-11-1916.			
			JMDavies	
			Lieut-Colonel R.F.A	
			Commanding 162nd Brigade R.F.A.,	

162nd BRIGADE R.F.A., NOVEMBER 1916.

Army Form C. 2118.

WAR DIARY
or
INTELLIGENCE SUMMARY
(Erase heading not required.)

Instructions regarding War Diaries and Intelligence Summaries are contained in F. S. Regs., Part II. and the Staff Manual respectively. Title Pages will be prepared in manuscript.

162 FA Bde

Place	Date	Hour	Summary of Events and Information	Remarks and references to Appendices
	Night 2/3		31st Division raided the enemy's trenches at 3 different points south of the sunken road east of HEBUTERNE in Square K.17. We assisted by putting up a flank barrage on front and support lines Owing to the heavy going of NO MAN'S LAND and opposition the raiding parties did not obtain their objective.	Brigade in action in positions between HEBUTERNE & SAILLY shown in last war diary
	Night 6/7		A raid was carried out by 31st Division (12th & 14th Yorks and Lancs). Three points of entry were to be made in the trenches south of the sunken road east of HEBUTERNE in Square K.17, we covering the right raiding party. There were two bombardments. One started at 1 Hour 50 minutes before ZERO and lasted 20 mins after which the raiding party crawled out into NO MAN'S LAND & got ready. The 2nd Bombardment started 2 mins before ZERO on the enemy's support lines for 4 minutes and the party entered the BOCHE trenches. Right raiding was the only party which managed to get in. They bombed the dug-outs, inflicting casualties on the enemy and secured 5 prisoners, one of whom died later on. The other parties were held up by machine gun fire.	
	Night 9/10		The whole area in the neighbourhood of SAILLY-AU-BOIS was heavily bombarded with gas shells about 3000 being fired between 11.5 p.m. and 2.20 a.m. We had no casualties.	
	13th	5.45 a.m.	On the 13th a General Offensive Operation was commenced along the 5th Army front. On our front (extending west of PUISIEUX and as far south as SERRE) held by 31st Division the objective was the German 1st and 2nd lines. Our Artillery preparation took the following form :- 27-10-1916 to 12-11-1916. (1). Wire cutting by deliberate shooting on an extensive scale on German Front, Reserve & support line wire. (2). Night firing consisting of bursts of fire at irregular intervals on gaps cut in the wire with the object of keeping them open and catching hostile wiring parties or patrols. Also on Communication Trenches, Approaches and	

Army Form C. 2118.

WAR DIARY
or
INTELLIGENCE SUMMARY
(Erase heading not required.)

162nd BRIGADE R.F.A., NOVEMBER 1916.

Instructions regarding War Diaries and Intelligence Summaries are contained in F. S. Regs., Part II. and the Staff Manual respectively. Title Pages will be prepared in manuscript.

Place	Date	Hour	Summary of Events and Information	Remarks and references to Appendices
	13th contd.		Trench Junctions in order to surprise, kill, and generally demoralize the Boche. Each night there was a quiet period of from 3 to 4 hours during which our patrols went out to examine the wire and report on the progress made in its destruction and any gaps found. The weather during the whole of the period was bad for observing and on 6 days no wire-cutting could be carried out at all, but, on the other days good progress was made and numerous lanes cut in the wire ready for the infantry assault. (3). Registration of all trenches and strong points. 10-11-16 to 12-11-16 (3 days). Special early morning bombardment from 5.45 a.m. to 6.0 a.m. It was hoped that the Boche, finding these bombardments regular and followed by no infantry attack would not know when to expect one, and would be, consequently, taken by surprise on the morning of attack. Our infantry (14th & 13th East Yorks) went over the parapet at ZERO 5.45 a.m. They were helped by a heavy mist which continued until late in the day. The going in NO MAN'S LAND proved very heavy but the German Front and Support trenches were taken on the Corps front from a point opposite JOHN COPSE to K.23.b.6.2. The enemy appeared to be taken by surprise and surrendered when it came to close fighting. The enemy's artillery barrage was not severe; opposition was chiefly caused by rifle and machine gun fire from positions in rear of the enemy's front and support lines. 129 prisoners were taken. It is believed that certain elements installed themselves in WALTER TRENCH and the southern portion of K.24.c. In accordance with Corps orders these trenches were evacuated in the evening. During the night strong patrols went out to facilitate the bringing in of wounded. This evacuation had to be made because the 3rd Division on our right was held up by mud and both our flanks were in mid-air. After midday the Boche put up a very heavy barrage on NO MAN'S LAND and also about 1000 yards behind line system. Our casualties	

Army Form C. 2118.

WAR DIARY
or
INTELLIGENCE SUMMARY
(Erase heading not required.)

162nd BRIGADE R.F.A., NOVEMBER 1916.

Instructions regarding War Diaries and Intelligence Summaries are contained in F. S. Regs., Part II. and the Staff Manual respectively. Title Pages will be prepared in manuscript.

Place	Date	Hour	Summary of Events and Information	Remarks and references to Appendices
	13th contd.		were very heavy on this front. The attack made down south and which was in co-operation with our attack was very successful. BEAUMONT-HAMEL was captured and an advance made on to the outskirts of BEAUCOURT over 3,000 prisoners being taken.	
	14th	6.5 a.m. 6.20 a.m.	to Bunny barrage was put up on enemy's support line in co-operation with an attack further down south.	
	Night 14th		51st Division took over responsibility for the line and "B" & "D" batteries received orders to pull out to their wagon lines.	
	15th		H.Q., and "A" & "C" Batteries moved to their wagon lines and Headquarters proceeded to LOUVENCOURT.	
	22nd		Brigade left LOUVENCOURT and Batteries their wagon lines at ST-LEGER-LES-AUTHIE- and the Brigade proceeded to VILLERS BOCAGE.	
	23rd		Brigade left VILLERS BOCAGE and proceeded to AIRAINES, Fourth Army area in order to rest.	
23-30			Brigade in rest at AIRAINES	

WAR DIARY

162nd BRIGADE R.F.A., NOVEMBER 1916.

Summary of Events and Information

CASUALTIES.

OFFICERS. Lieut E.G.Atterborough "A"/162 posted from "A"/162 to 33rd D.A.C., 9-11-1916.
2nd Lieut A.B.Neate posted to "B"/162 6-11-1916.

MEN.
Sick - 23 (18 evacuated).
Wounded - 13 (8 remained at Duty).
Killed - 5.
Joined - 19.
Posted away - 4.

HORSES.
Posted away - 21.
Joined - 22.
Deaths - 1. Killed.

2-12-1916.

M. Major R., for Lieut.-Col RFA
Commanding 162nd Brigade R.F.A.

Army Form C. 2118.

162nd Bd R.F.A. Vol/3

WAR DIARY
or
INTELLIGENCE SUMMARY

(Erase heading not required.)

162nd Brigade R.F.A.,

DECEMBER 1916.

Instructions regarding War Diaries and Intelligence Summaries are contained in F.S. Regs., Part II. and the Staff Manual respectively. Title Pages will be prepared in manuscript.

Place	Date	Hour	Summary of Events and Information	Remarks and references to Appendices
AIRAINES-SUR-SOMME.	1st.		Brigade still in rest at AIRAINES-SUR-SOMME.	
			Orders were received that we were to take over the French Line south of SAILLY SAILLISEL as far as BOUCHAVESNES by the 15th. We were to relieve the 127th French Regiment of Artillery. Two of our Infantry Brigades to be in the line from opposite BOUCHAVESNES to opposite RANCOURT, and to be covered by 33rd and 40th Divisional Artillery, 2 Brigades from each Divisional Artillery to be in the line and one at rest. The Artillery Brigades in the line to be 156th and 162nd from 33rd Div. Arty. and the 178th & 181st from 40th Div. Arty. 162nd Brigade went in on the right next to the French, their wagon lines situated at Camp No.21 on the MARICOURT-SUZANNE Road about 1 mile south of MARICOURT.	
	6th		"A" Battery complete moved from AIRAINES via ST.SAUVEUR and VAIRES-SUR-CORBIE to Camp No.14 situated on the BRAY-CORBIE Road 4 miles W. of BRAY.	
	8th		The Colonel, Battery Commanders, with telephonists proceeded direct by motor busses to P.C. GRANIERE, situated about 1 mile west of MAUREPAS, to take over Headquarters of the 127th French Regiment of Artillery. "C" Battery and Headquarters complete marched from AIRAINES to Camp No.14.	
	9th		"B" Battery complete marched to Camp No.14.	
	10th		"D" Battery complete marched to Camp No.14.	
	12th		2 Sections of "A" Battery and 2 Section of "C" Battery came into action in positions just west of the LE FOREST - CLERY Road about ½-w half way between those two villages.	

Army Form C. 2118.

WAR DIARY
or
INTELLIGENCE SUMMARY

(Erase heading not required.)

162nd Brigade R.F.A.,

Instructions regarding War Diaries and Intelligence Summaries are contained in F.S. Regs., Part II. and the Staff Manual respectively. Title Pages will be prepared in manuscript.

DECEMBER 1916.

Place	Date	Hour	Summary of Events and Information	Remarks and references to Appendices
	13th		2 Sections "B" Battery and remaining section of "C" Battery came into action.	
	14th		Remaining Section "A" Battery and remaining Section "B" Battery came into action. Headquarters established at P.C. CRANIERE, where also were the Headquarters of one of the Infantry Brigades Forward Exchange at AIGUILLE RAVINE taken over from French.	
	16th		2 Hows: came into action at the northern end of HOSPITAL WOOD.	
	21st		Information received that the undermentioned N.C.O's had been awarded the MILITARY MEDAL for acts of gallantry in the Field. 15390 Corpl. E.Williams. Headquarters. 37636 Sergt. F.A.Dawson. "A" Battery. 54091 A/Bdr. C.Lilley. "B" Battery. 23012 Sergt. R.T.Beebee. "D" Battery.	
	22nd		Remaining 2 Howitzers came into action.	
	28th		Information received that Capt. D.H.Pennant, the Medical Officer attached to Headquarters, had been awarded the Distinguished Service Order, and Lieut F.H.Warr of "D" Battery, the Military Cross for Acts of gallantry in the Field. The O.C., and Orderly Officer of 166th Brigade R.F.A. came up in advance to take over from the 156th Brigade R.F.A., and also established Headquarters at P.C. CRANIERE. The majority of the front that we covered could be observed but further north observation was impossible. No trenches behind the enemy's support lines could be observed owing to the steep valley running down towards MOISLAINS.	

2449 Wt. W14957/M90 750,000 1/16 J.B.C. & A. Forms/C.2118/12.

Army Form C. 2118.

162nd BRIGADE R.F.A.,

WAR DIARY
or
INTELLIGENCE SUMMARY

(Erase heading not required.)

DECEMBER 1916.

Instructions regarding War Diaries and Intelligence Summaries are contained in F. S. Regs., Part II. and the Staff Manual respectively. Title Pages will be prepared in manuscript.

Place	Date	Hour	Summary of Events and Information	Remarks and references to Appendices

			The objectives of the 162nd Brigade R.F.A., were the enemy trenches on the BOUCHAVESNES ridge from the south to the west corner of the MOISLAINS WOOD. The 156th Brigade R.F.A., covered thence as far north to and including a portion of the BOIS ST PIERRE VAAST. Trenches PALLAS, FRITZ, BREMEN, HALICZ, DROSSEN being front and support line trenches in the area. Very little infantry action during the period. Hostile Artillery fire was directed more on back areas than on the front trench system. Hostile back areas, including Communication Trenches, Tracks, roads, command posts and located batteries being chiefly engaged by us. Weather bad, much rain, and the area a sea of mud. Brigade O.P. was established on the ridge east of the AIGUILLE Valley giving a clear view of the hostile system.
			
			------------oOo------------
			
			C A S U A L T I E S.
			
			Officers :- 2nd Lieut J.V.Macartney-Filgate Joined 11-12-1916.
			
			Men:- Killed - Nil.
			      Wounded - Nil.
			      Sick - 41.
			      Posted Away - 5.
			
			Horses:- Posted Away - 36 (Evacuated to M.V.S).
			        Joined - 58.
			        Deaths - 1 shot.
			
			2-1-1917. Lieut-Col, R.F.A.,
			                                                Commanding 162nd Brigade R.F.A.,	

Army Form C. 2118.

162nd BRIGADE, R.F.A.,

WAR DIARY
or
INTELLIGENCE SUMMARY

(Erase heading not required.)

JANUARY, 1916.

Instructions regarding War Diaries and Intelligence Summaries are contained in F. S. Regs., Part II. and the Staff Manual respectively. Title Pages will be prepared in manuscript.

Vol/4

Place	Date	Hour	Summary of Events and Information	Remarks and references to Appendices
	1st		Brigade still in action in positions as shown in War Diary for December, 1915.	
	14th		Re-organisation of Divisional Artilleries. A Section of "D"/156 Howitzer Battery posted to "D"/162nd Brigade Howitzer Battery, forming a 6-4.5" How: Btty.	
	15th to 22nd		Brigade withdrew to its wagon lines, i.e., at Camp 21, west of the MARICOURT-SUZANNE road. Advantage was taken of the frozen roads to get up 400 rds per gun at the new gun positions.	
	23rd & 24th		Brigade went into action again in positions E. of FEUILLERES, on the south side of the river SOMME and the CANAL-DU-NORD, being the first British Artillery on this side of the river since the earlier stages of the war. "C" Battery were situated nearest the river between BUSCOURT Cemetery and the river. "A" Battery were located just south of the Cemetery. "D" Battery were about 200 yards in front of "A" Battery under the bank of a hill. "B" Battery had 4 guns in action S.E. of these positions i.e., half way between BUSCOURT and a line drawn S.E. to a corner of the river. They had a detached enfilade section about 700 yds S. of FEUILLERES and behind CHAPTER WOOD. just N.W. of FLECOURT Brigade Headquarters were situated about 100 yds behind "C" Battery in an old Boche 2nd Line Trench. The choice of Battery positions in this area was very difficult owing to the fact that clear days gave the Boche direct observation over the whole countryside from MT.ST.QUENTIN. The Brigade formed a sub-group under Col. NEVINSON of the 23rd Div Brigade R.F.A., 8th Division. The front covered by the Brigade was from the river SOMME up to a point 300 yds N. of the FEUILLAUCOURT-CLERY SUR SOMME Road, the enemy trenches running from the river SOMME to the W. corner of LIEBKLOSI WOOD - FRICKLES WOOD - and thence in a N.E., direction.	

Army Form C. 2118.

2. 162nd BRIGADE R.F.A.,

WAR DIARY

INTELLIGENCE SUMMARY

JANUARY, 1917, contd.

(Erase heading not required.)

Instructions regarding War Diaries and Intelligence Summaries are contained in F. S. Regs., Part II. and the Staff Manual respectively. Title Pages will be prepared in manuscript.

Place	Date	Hour	Summary of Events and Information	Remarks and references to Appendices
	21st		The 35rd Division had two Infantry Brigades in the line, each having two battalions. These were covered by two Groups, (1). Col STEWART O.C., 156th Brigade R.F.A., commanded the Left Group consisting of the 156th and 14th Brigades R.F.A., and (2). Col NEVINSON O.C., 53rd Brigade R.F.A., commanded the Right Group consisting of the 53rd Brigade R.F.A., and ourselves. O.Ps. These were established on the south bank of the canal about 1800 yds due east of HAILE, which gave a fine enfilade view of the front we covered and also an extensive back area view of the country from PERONNE in the south, AT-ST-QUENTIN, FEUILLAUCOURT, and ALLAINES and along the PARIS-LILLE Road in the direction of LURLU. Col HARRIS, D.S.O., took over command of the Right Group. During the period in action hostile artillery fire was on the whole quiet but our infantry were considerably worried by "Minnies" and Rifle Grenades. Through prompt retaliation from the batteries their activities were reduced to a minimum. Weather conditions during the period in action were abnormal, snow covering the ground the whole time, and on most nights the thermometer registering between 15 & 17 degrees below freezing point.	

Army Form C. 2118.

WAR DIARY
of
INTELLIGENCE SUMMARY
(Erase heading not required.)

162nd BRIGADE R.F.A.,   JANUARY, 1917

Place	Date	Hour	Summary of Events and Information	Remarks and references to Appendices
			C A S U A L T I E S.	

Officers :-
2nd. Capt. T.St.F.Bunbury wounded. Invalided to England 11th.
6th. 2nd Lieut N.K.Brooks "A"/162 evacuated sick.
14th. Capt J.R.McCallum and 2nd Lieut A.H.Whiting posted to "D"/162 from "D"/156 on re-organisation.
15th. 2nd Lieuts. W.H.T.Green and F.D.Warren posted to "D"/162.
19th. 2nd Lieut B.S.M.Paterson, "C"/162 evacuated sick.
22nd. 2nd Lieut L.E.Brown-Greaves 20th Hussars posted as Officer in charge of Brigade Wagon Lines.
29th. 2nd Lieut C.Bartholomew posted to "A"/162.

Men :-
2 Wounded and evacuated on 26th & 27th respectively.
45 admitted to hospital sick.
20 discharged from hospital to duty.
4 posted away (To Base).
60 posted from "D"/156 to "D"/162 on re-organisation. 14th.
1 Farr.Sergt posted from Base.

HORSES :-
45 posted to "D"/162 from "D"/156 on re-organisation 14th.

and struck off.

O.Marris
Lieut-Colonel, R.F.A.,
Commanding 162nd Brigade R.F.A.,

Army Form C. 2118.

WAR DIARY
or
INTELLIGENCE SUMMARY
(Erase heading not required.)

FEBRUARY 1917.

162nd Brigade R.F.A.,

Instructions regarding War Diaries and Intelligence Summaries are contained in F.S. Regs., Part II. and the Staff Manual respectively. Title Pages will be prepared in manuscript.

Place	Date	Hour	Summary of Events and Information	Remarks and references to Appendices
	1st.		Brigade still in action South of the river SOMME at BUSCOURT.	
			"A" Battery pulled out of action preparatory to going into rest at VAUX. The 6 guns were taken to the northern part of MARRIERES WOOD, 1000 yds West of BOUCHAVESNES, there left under a guard and eventually handed over to 135th Battery, 32nd Bde, R.F.A.,	
	2nd.		A bombardment was carried out by Heavy and Field Artillery on enemy trenches from RANCOURT-BOUCHAVESNES-PERONNE Road north. We assisted on the flanks.	
	3rd.		"B" Battery brought two guns for wire cutting into action at a point where the canal lock meets the river on the southern side of the SOMME south east of CLERY-SUR-SOMME. These two guns had formerly served as the enfilade section just N.E., of FLAUCOURT and this position was now occupied by a Section of "C" Battery that had moved from a position east of CHAPTER WOOD 800 yards south of FEUILLERES. This latter position was relinquished. Another wire cutting section came into action 200 yds north east of CLERY-SUR-SOMME by the 33rd Brigade R.F.A., of this Group.	
	6th		"D" Battery moved out to rest at SAILLY-LE-SEC. 2 of their Howitzers were left in position and taken over by a Section of the 55th How: Battery, 33rd Brigade R.F.A.,	
	7th		We assisted in a Raid carried out by LEFT GROUP at a point where the German trenches cross the BOUCHAVESNES-PERONNE Road by putting up a dummy barrage round FRECKLES WOOD.	
	10th		The enemy front was bombarded by Heavy and Field Artillery from the SOMME to a point 1500 yards south of BOUCHAVESNES nearly up	

Army Form C. 2118.

WAR DIARY
or
INTELLIGENCE SUMMARY

(Erase heading not required.)

FEBRUARY 1917

162nd Brigade R.F.A.,

Instructions regarding War Diaries and Intelligence Summaries are contained in F. S. Regs., Part II. and the Staff Manual respectively. Title Pages will be prepared in manuscript.

Place	Date	Hour	Summary of Events and Information	Remarks and references to Appendices
	February 1917. 10th (contd).		to the RANCOURT-BOUCHAVESNES-PERONNE Road. The bombardment commenced at 1 p.m. and at 6 p.m. it was reduced but continued throughout the night, becoming intense at 6 p.m. 6.15 p.m. 6.15 a.m. 11th and lasting for 20 minutes.	
	13/14		A raid was carried out on the Brigade front by the 4th Suffolks, on trenches known as PEKLY BULGE roughly just south of the CLERY-sur-SOMME - FEUILLAUCOURT Road. The raid lasted 30 minutes No prisoners were brought back to our trenches; 4 were secured but these, with their escort of 2 were killed by an enemy Heavy Trench Mortar whilst crossing NO MAN'S LAND. Much damage was done to the hostile trenches and 2 dug-outs were blown in. Our casualties were 3 Killed and 5 Wounded.	
	17th		Bombardment carried out by Field and Heavy Artillery on enemy front from the CLERY-sur-SOMME Road up to a point 1700 yards south of BOUCHAVESNES. Bombardment commenced at 7.30 a.m. and continued up to 1-10 p.m. and was then intense for 15 minutes. At 6.10 p.m. intense fire was again opened for 5 minutes.	
	20th		"D" Battery came into action again from rest into their old position.	
	21/22/23		"A" Battery came into action again from rest into their old position bringing in a Section each night.	
	21st		On morning of 21st the Artillery Arrangements for the defence of the front were altered: Right Group being covered by 162nd Bde R.F.A., with the assistance of "C"/156 and 55th How: Battery. Major J.D.Belgrave, D.S.O., assumed temporary command of the Right Group during the absence on leave of Lieut-Colonel O.M. Harris, D.S.O. "A" Zones were altered as follows :- "C"/162 and "A"/162 with 55th How: Btty covered Right Battalion. "B"/162 and "C"/156 with "D"/162 Hows: " " Left " .	

Army Form C. 2118.

WAR DIARY
or
INTELLIGENCE SUMMARY

(Erase heading not required.)

162nd Brigade R.F.A.

FEBRUARY 1917.

Instructions regarding War Diaries and Intelligence Summaries are contained in F. S. Regs., Part II. and the Staff Manual respectively. Title Pages will be prepared in manuscript.

Place	Date	Hour	Summary of Events and Information	Remarks and references to Appendices
	February 1917 23rd		One gun of "A" Battery was placed in position vacated by wire cutting guns of 33rd Brigade R.F.A., 200 yards east of CLERY-sur-SOMME.	
	27/28		We supported the 2nd Worcesters in a raid. Official report was as follows :- "The 2nd Worcester Regt. carried out a successful raid last night (27/28) on PERLY BULGE about I.7.b.3.3. The raid was made in two phases ZERO for 1st phase being at 8.40 p.m. and for 2nd phase at 1 a.m. 6 dug-outs were bombed and at least 36 of the enemy are known to have been killed in hand to hand fighting in the trenches. 7 prisoners were captured in first attack and 15 in the 2nd including one UNTER-OFFICER. They mostly belong to 2nd Guards Grenadier Regt, 2nd Guards Regt Division. This identification is of great value as it was not known that the 29th Division had been relieved." The G.O.C., of 100th Infantry Brigade (i.e., General Baird) was delighted with the artillery barrage in both cases. ---------o0o---------	

Army Form C. 2118.

WAR DIARY
or
INTELLIGENCE SUMMARY

(Erase heading not required.)

FEBRUARY 1917. 162nd Brigade R.F.A.,

Instructions regarding War Diaries and Intelligence Summaries are contained in F.S. Regs., Part II. and the Staff Manual respectively. Title Pages will be prepared in manuscript.

Place	Date	Hour	Summary of Events and Information	Remarks and references to Appendices
	February 1917 23rd		One gun of "A" Battery was placed in position vacated by wire cutting guns of 33rd Brigade R.F.A., 200 yards east of CLERY-sur-SOMME.	
	27/28		We supported the 2nd Worcesters in a raid. Official report was as follows :- "The 2nd Worcester Regt. carried out a successful raid last night (27/28) on PEKLY BULGE about I.7.b.3.3. The raid was made in two phases ZERO for 1st phase being at 8.40 p.m. and for 2nd phase.at 1 a.m. 6 dug-outs were bombed and at least 36 of the enemy are known to have been killed in hand to hand fighting in the trenches. 7 prisoners were captured in first attack and 15 in the 2nd including one UNTER-OFFICER. They mostly belong to 2nd Guards Grenadier Regt, 2nd Guards Regt Division. This identification is of great value as it was not known that the 29th Division had been relieved." The G.O.C., of 100th Infantry Brigade (i.e., General Baird) was delighted with the artillery barrage in both cases.

---0o0--- | |

Army Form C. 2118.

WAR DIARY
INTELLIGENCE SUMMARY
(Erase heading not required.)

162nd Brigade R.F.A.

FEBRUARY 1917.

Instructions regarding War Diaries and Intelligence Summaries are contained in F.S. Regs., Part II. and the Staff Manual respectively. Title Pages will be prepared in manuscript.

Place	Date	Hour	Summary of Events and Information	Remarks and references to Appendices
			C A S U A L T I E S.	

Officers :-
Capt. J.R.McCallum posted to "C"/93 Brigade R.F.A.,   6-2-17
Lieut. T.R.Jackson posted to H.Q., 33rd Div. Arty.   7-2-17
2nd Lieut B.S.M.Paterson invalided to England sick on 7-2-17
 and struck off vide G.H.Q., D.A.G., List No.669 of 9th.
2nd Lieut R.C.Norton posted to "C" Battery   14-2-17
Lieut M.M.I.Body re-joined "B" Battery   15-2-17
2nd Lieut V.H.Westerby posted to R.F.C., as an observer 15-2-17

Men :-
Killed or died of wounds.   Nil.
Wounded in action.   Nil.
Admitted to Hospital sick - 60.
Discharged from Hospital to duty.- 17.
Posted away - 6.
Joined, reinforcements - 75.

J. Belgrave   Major R.F.A.,
Commanding 162nd Brigade R.F.A.,

Army Form C. 2118.

WAR DIARY
or
INTELLIGENCE SUMMARY
(*Erase heading not required.*)

162 Bde RFA Vol 16

Instructions regarding War Diaries and Intelligence Summaries are contained in F. S. Regs., Part II. and the Staff Manual respectively. Title Pages will be prepared in manuscript.

Place	Date	Hour	Summary of Events and Information	Remarks and references to Appendices
	MARCH, 1917. 1st.		Brigade still in action at BUSCOURT.	
	9th.		Brigade left BUSCOURT after handing over to 178th Brigade.R.F.A 40th Division, and proceeded to Wagon Lines at ECLUSIER.	
	10th.		Brigade left ECLUSIER at about 12.30 p.m. and marched to SAILLM-LE-SEC via BRAY-sur-SOMME.	
	17th.		One half of 166th Brigade R.F.A. Headquarters (disbanded on account of the re-organisation 14.1.17.) posted to this Brigade.	
	24th.		O.C., Brigade and Battery Commanders proceeded from SAILLY-LE-SEC to prospective positions in ARRAS.	
	25th.		Brigade left SAILLY-LE-SEC at about 6 a.m. and proceeded to TALMAS via MERICOURT L'ABBE - HEILLY - FRANVILLERS - BEHENCOURT - MONTIGNY - MOLLIENS-au-BOIS - PIERREGOT.	
	26th.		Advance parties of 1 Officer and 20 Men per Battery, Orderly Officer and Officers Mess of H.Q., left TALMAS and proceeded by Motor Lorries to ARRAS, arriving there at about 11.30 p.m.	
	27th.		Brigade left TALMAS about 8 a.m. and proceeded to HEUZECOURT via NAOURS - WARGNIES - HAVERNAS - CANAPLES - BERNAVILLE -.	
	28th.		Brigade left HEUZECOURT about 12 noon and proceeded to PETIT BOURET and GRAND BOURET-sur-CANCHE., about 1½ miles West of FREVENT., via BEALCOURT - BEAUVOIR RIVIERE - WAVANS - BOIS D'AUXI - VACQUERIE-1e-BOUCQ - LIGNY-sur-CANCHE.	
			Major A.B.VanStraubenzee O.C., "C"/162 and Major V.Benett-Stanford O.C., "B"/162 wounded by shell fire in rear of the Station at ARRAS and evacuated	

2449 Wt. W14957/M90 750,000 1/16 J.B.C. & A. Forms/C.2118/12.

Army Form C. 2118.

WAR DIARY
or
INTELLIGENCE SUMMARY

(Erase heading not required.)

Instructions regarding War Diaries and Intelligence Summaries are contained in F. S. Regs., Part II. and the Staff Manual respectively. Title Pages will be prepared in manuscript.

Place	Date	Hour	Summary of Events and Information	Remarks and references to Appendices
MARCH 1917	(Contd)			
	29th.		Brigade left PETIT and GRAND BOURET-sur-CANCHE at about 7 a.m. and proceeded to DUISANS via REBREUVE - ETREE WAMIN - LIENCOURT - AVESNES-le-COMTE - HABARCQ - AGNEZ-lez-DUISANS. Wagon Lines were established just clear of the southern end of DUISANS. Headquarters left DUISANS about 5 p.m. and proceeded to Gun Line at ARRAS were Headquarters were at 34 RUE DES CAPUCINS.	
	30th.		The remainder of Gunners at Wagon Lines came up to Battery Positions. The guns remained at the Wagon Lines.	
	31st.		"A"/162 brought 2 wire cutting guns into action in a position in the garden of a house on the outskirts of ARRAS. Their task was to cut wire just south of the river SCARPE on the enemy's 2nd and 3rd Lines. ------ The following awards were made during the month for acts of gallantry in the Field. Lieut-Col O.M.Harris, D.S.O., Chevalier Of the Order of the Crown 14066 Bdr. H.GILL, "C" Battery Military Medal. (of Italy). 15130 Gr. A.W.ERSSER, "B" Battery Military Medal. 22439 Cpl. F.M.HAYMAN, "A" Battery Military Medal.	

Army Form C. 2118.

WAR DIARY
162nd Brigade R.F.A.
INTELLIGENCE SUMMARY

(Erase heading not required.)

Place	Date	Hour	Summary of Events and Information	Remarks and references to Appendices
	March 1917	continued.	C A S U A L T I E S.	
	30-3-17		Officers :- Major A.B.VanStraubenzee, "C"/162 wounded 28-3-1917. Major V.Benetto Stanford, "B"/162 wounded 28-3-1917. Capt. H.C.Cory, "B"/162 Admitted to Hospital 29-3-1917. Capt. A.E.G.Champion, "D"/162 Admitted to Hospital 20-3-1917. 2nd Lieut G.Coleman "A"/162, Joined from Base 25-3-1917. (Capt. E.G.Lutyens and Capt W.G.Pringle temporarily attached to ("B" and "D" Batteries respectively for duty from 156th Bde RFA Major J.D.Belgrave, D.S.O.; Posted to XIVth Corps Headquarters as G.S.O., 2nd Grade, 20-3-1917. ("D"/162). Lieut H.A.C.Walton, "D"/162 posted to 33rd D.A.C., 12-3-17. 2nd Lieut A.H.Whiting, "D"/162 posted to 33rd D.A.C., 6-3-17. 2nd Lieut W.E.Harrison, "B"/162 Joined from Base 10-3-1917 2nd Lieut C.W.Almack, "D"/162 Joined from "D"/156 25-3-1917. Men:- Wounded - (1 on 3rd. Killed or died of wounds - NIL. (3 on 5th. Admitted to Hospital - 22. Discharged from Hospital to duty - 7. Joined - 55. Posted away - 4.	

Signature
Lieut-Col R.F.A.,
Commanding 162nd Brigade R.F.A.,

Army Form C. 2118.

WAR DIARY
INTELLIGENCE SUMMARY
(Erase heading not required.)

162nd BRIGADE R.F.A.,
APRIL 1917.

Instructions regarding War Diaries and Intelligence Summaries are contained in F. S. Regs., Part II. and the Staff Manual respectively. Title Pages will be prepared in manuscript.

Place	Date	Hour	Summary of Events and Information	Remarks and references to Appendices
	1st		All remaining guns of the Brigade were brought into action, "A" and "D" Batteries into positions on the right of the road leading from the Octroi of ARRAS towards ST. NICHOLAS, and "B" and "C" Batteries into positions to the East of ST. NICHOLAS.	
	2nd		A bad blizzard raged over the area from the effects of which many horses died - 7 in this Brigade - and 30 in the Divisional Artillery.	
	4th		Armoured cable laid through the sewers of ARRAS to "B" and "C" Batteries and completed.	
	5th		Armoured cable laid to "A" and "D" Batteries. Up to this date Headquarters were in communication with the batteries by D.III wire.	
	8th		Wagon Lines moved from DUISANS to advanced positions just outside ARRAS on the left of the road running from ARRAS to ARRAH.	
	9th		Battle of ARRAS. On the 4th, 5th, 6th, 7th, & 8th insts., the 33rd and 15th Divisional Artilleries with "A" and "H" Groups, VIth Corps Heavy Artillery in support, bombarded the enemy front opposite that held by the 15th Division Infantry in preparation for a general aggresive operation. South of ARRAS the enemy had fallen back to the HINDENBURG line and it was estimated that 3 enemy battalions held the line from TILLOY-LES-MAFFAINES to the river SCARPE. Opposite the 15th Div. front was the 10th Grenadier Regt., 11th Div. At 5.30 a.m., in a drizzling rain, the Infantry assault was launched by VIth Corps on this front, with the VIIth and XVIIth Corps respectively on our right and left. The German front system, which was the first objective, was stormed and rapidly carried by the 44th and 45th Infantry Brigades A number of prisoners were taken.	

2449 Wt. W14957/Mgo 750,000 1/16 J.B.C. & A. Forms/C.2118/12.

Army Form C. 2118.

WAR DIARY
or
INTELLIGENCE SUMMARY
(Erase heading not required.)

162nd BRIGADE R.F.A.,   APRIL 1918.

Instructions regarding War Diaries and Intelligence Summaries are contained in F. S. Regs., Part II. and the Staff Manual respectively. Title Pages will be prepared in manuscript.

Place	Date	Hour	Summary of Events and Information	Remarks and references to Appendices
	9th contd.		The German 2nd System was the 2nd Objective and this was also assaulted by the 44th and 45th Infantry Brigades. Stiff opposition was met at the RAILWAY TRIANGLE, 1000 yards E. of BLANGY, where the enemy were bringing strong machine gun fire to bear. Our barrage fire had passed over the embankment without harming the machine gunners. The barrage was brought back towards our troops again until it rested exactly over the embankment, when every living being was wiped out. This strategical position was finally taken by our Infantry with only 3 men wounded. Tanks co-operated in this attack and rendered valuable assistance. More prisoners were taken. The next phase was the attack on the German third system by the 45th Infantry Brigade who, during the taking of the first two systems of defence, had issued forth from the cellars and sewers of ARRAS into a position of assembly in the German front line and advanced to the attack. Our batteries, directly the 2nd system had fallen, advanced by Sections to forward positions on the right of the road mid-way between ARRAS and BLANGY. The 2nd Section of Batteries did not advance until the 1st Section in its new position had registered. The 3rd Section advanced as soon as the 2nd opened fire. In this way a protective barrage of 4 guns per battery was maintained during the advance on the German 3rd System, which was finally reached at nightfall, the batteries having again advanced to positions near the RAILWAY TRIANGLE, "A" Battery on the Eastern side, "B", "C", and "D" Batteries on the western side. Brigade Headquarters occupied a dug-out by the bridge of the RAILWAY TRIANGLE. The German third system was the final objective for the day and was the ridge running North and South N.W. of MONCHY-LE-PREUX. The Infantry established posts on the northern slopes of ORANGE HILL. Many prisoners and guns were taken, and a considerable number of German dead were left on the captured ground.	

WAR DIARY or INTELLIGENCE SUMMARY

(*Erase heading not required.*)

Army Form C. 2118.

162nd BRIGADE R.F.A.,

APRIL 1916.

Instructions regarding War Diaries and Intelligence Summaries are contained in F.S. Regs., Part II. and the Staff Manual respectively. Title Pages will be prepared in manuscript.

Place	Date	Hour	Summary of Events and Information	Remarks and references to Appendices
	10th		Batteries still in action at the RAILWAY TRIANGLE. At 2.30 p.m. orders were received to advance to positions 1000 yards south of FEUCHY. Owing to the very heavy going of the roads and congestion of traffic, Batteries did not get into action until 9 a.m., 11th. A certain amount of firing was done in registration. Hostile fire was very weak.	
	11th		37th Div. Infantry who had been in reserve took up the attack and stormed MONCHY-LE-PREUX from the North East and after severe fighting the village was taken. The Cavalry co-operated and made three charges. Our line advanced thereby some 400 yards to the East of MONCHY-LE-PREUX and up to the river SCARPE. Battery and H.Q., wagon Lines moved up to a position 500 yards behind the guns. Both our flanks also tried to advance but were not able to make any appreciable progress. The Army on our left had captured and held the VIMY RIDGE with many prisoners. The Army on our right had captured BULLECOURT and RIENCOURT, but were later driven out and retired to their original position.	
	12th		29th Division on our right and 9th on our left tried to advance but were unsuccessful. Headquarters moved from the RAILWAY TRIANGLE to an old German 5.9" Gun-pit in FEUCHY.	
	13th		Batteries and Wagon Lines during the morning were heavily shelled. It was decided to hold the ground already gained until the flanks came up, and accordingly Battery Wagon Lines were ordered back to ARRAS. Pack animals were stationed at the RAILWAY TRIANGLE. During the night Batteries and H.Q., wagon line were heavily gas shelled.	

162nd BRIGADE R.F.A.,

WAR DIARY

INTELLIGENCE SUMMARY

APRIL 1917.

Army Form C. 2118.

(Erase heading not required.)

Place	Date	Hour	Summary of Events and Information	Remarks and references to Appendices
	14th		The enemy delivered a violent counter attack on MONCHY-LE-PREUX which was broken up by our artillery fire.	
	23rd		An attack was made in the early hours of the morning to capture BAYONET TRENCH to the N.E. of MONCHY-LE-PREUX and to straighten out the re-entrant at this part of the front. 17th Div Infantry made the attack which failed owing to enfilade machine gun fire from ROEUX and from both sides of the river SCARPE. Three attempts were made in all.	
	28th		An operation was carried out to capture those portions of BAYONET and RIFLE TRENCHES still in the hands of the enemy. Infantry attack began at 4.25 a.m. when 12th and 33rd D.A., Batteries put up a protective barrage. Observation was rendered difficult by mist and smoke shell but at 5.58 a.m. the first objective was reported gained. The Left Battalion was held up at this point by heavy Machine Gun fire, but the Right advanced accordingly to plan and was reported to have reached the second objective. At 6.40 a.m. owing to the Division on our left being held up, a smoke barrage was put down on the south side of the river SCARPE. Early in the day our Howitzers were turned on to troublesome Machine Guns and during the rest of the day the batteries were fully occupied with protective barrage and smashing enemy efforts to mass for counter attacks. At 11.30 a.m. an attempt was made to consolidate the line then held but failed owing to heavy machine gun fire across the river SCARPE. The enemy's artillery opened a light barrage of 10.5 c.m. and 7.7 c.m shells three minutes after our own barrage commenced and about 7.30 a.m. a heavier barrage was put down on BAYONET TRENCH but generally speaking hostile shelling was slight until 10 a.m. when things became livelier. Summing up, BAYONET TRENCH was captured in its entirety, but only a portion of RIFLE TRENCH was taken. The infantry	

Army Form C. 2118.

WAR DIARY
or
INTELLIGENCE SUMMARY

(Erase heading not required.)

162nd BRIGADE R.F.A., APRIL 1917.

Instructions regarding War Diaries and Intelligence Summaries are contained in F. S. Regs., Part II. and the Staff Manual respectively. Title Pages will be prepared in manuscript.

Place	Date	Hour	Summary of Events and Information	Remarks and references to Appendices
	28th contd.		advance was greatly impeded throughout by machine gun fire. It would appear from Observation and Intelligence that the enemy had concentrated in considerable force on this front and it was probably due to the excellence of the work done by F.O.O's and Batteries that the many counter attacks attempted had been smashed before they could come to fruition.	
	29th		Line of posts established and front generally consolidated by Infantry.	
	30th		An attack was carried out at 3.0.a.m. with a view to capturing the remaining portion of RIFLE TRENCH still in enemy hands. At 3.1 a.m. batteries put up a protective barrage on their S.O.S. lines. This attack also failed.	
			The following awards were made by the Corps Commander for acts of gallantry on the 9th in the battle of ARRAS. (VI Corps Routine Order 2042 of 29-4-17).	
			26990 Bdr. W.B.Mason, "D" Battery. 2417 Gr. J.Shilcock, "A" Battery. 13203 Gr. W.Ellerbeck, "B" Battery. 15184 Dr. C.G.Lytton, "C" Battery.	Military Medal

Army Form C. 2118.

WAR DIARY
or
INTELLIGENCE SUMMARY

(Erase heading not required.)

162nd BRIGADE R.F.A.,   APRIL 1917.

Instructions regarding War Diaries and Intelligence Summaries are contained in F. S. Regs., Part II. and the Staff Manual respectively. Title Pages will be prepared in manuscript.

Place	Date	Hour	Summary of Events and Information	Remarks and references to Appendices
Battle Casualties.			C A S U A L T I E S.	
			(Killed in action. 1 Officer 7 Other Ranks.	
			(Died of Wounds. 1 Other Rank.	
			(Wounded and evacuated. 4 Officers 33 Other Ranks.	
			(Wounded (remained at duty). 6 Other Ranks.	
			Sick and evacuated. 54.	
			Discharged from Hospital. 10.	
			Posted to Brigade. 42.	
			Posted away from Brigade. 3. (For Munitions Work).	
			Officer Casualties.	
			2nd Lieut N.S.Bostock Killed in action 22-4-17.)	
			2nd Lieut A.B.Meate. Died Of Wounds. 22-4-17.)	
			2nd Lieut W.E.Harrison. Wounded in action 9-4-17.) Battle
			2nd Lieut S.N.Beall. Wounded in action 23-4-17.) Casualties
			Capt. W.M.I.Body. Wounded in action 23-4-17.)	
			Major V.Benett-Stanford. Wounded in action 23-4-17.)	
			Posted to Bde.	
			2nd Lieut F.C.Rose. 14-4-17.	
			2nd Lieut S.N.Beall. 14-4-17.	
			2nd Lieut R.C.Essex. 23-4-17.	
			2nd Lieut E.Wimshurst. 25-4-17.	
			Major W.P.Colfox. 3-4-17.	

[signature] Lieut-Col R.F.A.,
Commanding 162nd Brigade R.F.A.,

Army Form C. 2118.

WAR DIARY
or
INTELLIGENCE SUMMARY

(Erase heading not required.)

162nd Brigade. R.F.A.

MAY - 1917.

Instructions regarding War Diaries and Intelligence Summaries are contained in F. S. Regs., Part II. and the Staff Manual respectively. Title Pages will be prepared in manuscript.

162 Bde R.F.A 33
Vol 18

Place	Date	Hour	Summary of Events and Information	Remarks and references to Appendices
	May. 1st.		**Operations** An attack had been prepared with the object of gaining the whole of RIFLE TRENCH - it was found, however, impossible to carry out the scheme, but we managed to gain about 65 yards more of this Trench which we still hold.	Sul.
	3rd.	3.45 a.m.	The 1st., 3rd and 5th Armies attacked on the front between ARLEUX EN GOHELLE and the East of BULLECOURT, and progress was made at many points.	Sul.
			On this front the 36th and 37th Infantry Brigades attacked, supported by the 53rd and 12th Divisional Artilleries and the VIth Corps Heavy Artillery.	Sul.
			The advance was met with very heavy Machine Gun fire and an artillery barrage, but our front waves succeeded in forcing their way to about the line 1.25 d.7.9. - GUN TRENCH. Here the situation became obscure as did the position of our right flank. A very heavy machine gun barrage was put down by the enemy and it was found impossible to communicate with our leading troops.	Sul.
			At 10 A.M. a party of Germans entered SCABBARD TRENCH from the North and bombed our men out as far as its junction with NEW TRENCH. The 18 pounders kept up a protective barrage over the 1st objective to save any of our Infantry who had already reached there.	
		12.10 p.m.	A new bombardment and attack was organised and at 2.10 p.m. two companies of the 7th Royal Sussex Regiment assaulted the Trench, about 50 germans at once ran out of the Northern end of the trench and fled down the bank towards the East. Another party estimated about 500 also left the banks in 1.25.d. and made for the road Junction at 1.25 d.7.9. Artillery opened on both parties with good results.	R.C.
			About 2.15 p.m. the enemy counter-attacked our positions in SCABBARD TRENCH but was driven off with losses - leaving 1 Officer 25 men and 2 Machine Guns in our hands. Some total of 2 Officers and 77 Other Ranks were taken prisoners, we also captured 3 Machine Guns.	Sul. Sul.

Army Form C. 2118.

WAR DIARY
or
INTELLIGENCE SUMMARY

162nd Brigade. R.F.A.

MAY -1917 (contd.) (Erase heading not required.)

Place	Date	Hour	Summary of Events and Information	Remarks and references to Appendices
	3rd (Contd.)		During the afternoon various targets presented themselves and were dealt with, especially Infantry collecting behind KEEPING COPSE and running in small batches to CARTRIDGE TRENCH. A good view of counter-attacks on the 4th Divisions front were obtained and these attacks were effectively dealt with. On our right the attack on ROEUX, north of the river SCARPE failed. Left.	Enc.
			On our Right all objectives were gained including the village of CHERISI, but heavy counter-attacks drove our troops back to the west of that village which again fell into the enemy's hands.	Enc
			The 1st Army captured FRESNOI and all its objectives north of OPPY. An attack on OPPY, however, failed, and none of the objectives south of it were gained.	Enc
			The 5th army advanced beyond BULLECOURT but were forced back and the village is now held by the enemy.	Enc
			We have captured the HINDENBURG line to the East of BULLECOURT and also most of the line to the West.	Enc.
	4th.		Consolidated all gains.	Enc
	11/12th		Our Artillery assisted in an attack made by the 4th Division on our left - North of the River,with the object of taking and holding CHEMICAL WORKS and ROEUX CEMETERY. At 7.30 p.m. we opened a very heavy barrage with a density of 1-18pdr. for every 7 yards front. All objectives were gained and 300 prisoners taken.	Enc'
			At 6 a.m. 12th we put a protective barrage on the North-Western end of ROEUX down to the river and the Infantry assaulted and furthered their position E. of the river. 150 prisoners were taken.	Enc

Army Form C. 2118.

WAR DIARY
or
INTELLIGENCE SUMMARY

(Erase heading not required.)

162nd Brigade. R.F.A.

Instructions regarding War Diaries and Intelligence Summaries are contained in F.S. Regs., Part II. and the Staff Manual respectively. Title Pages will be prepared in manuscript. MAY -1917 (Conted).

Place	Date	Hour	Summary of Events and Information	Remarks and references to Appendices
	12/13th		The 3rd and 12th Divisions received Orders to capture and consolidate DEVIL'S TRENCH. The objective of the 12th Division (36th and 37th Infantry Brigades) was that portion of DEVIL'S TRENCH running North from BIT LANE to HARNESS LANE. (inclusive.) At Zero the Artillery put up a Barrage on DEVIL'S TRENCH - and 3 minutes later lifted to allow our Troops to assault. The barrage density was one gun to every 10 yards. The attack was held up by heavy Machine Gun and Rifle fire from both flanks - viz:- from GUN and DEVIL'S TRENCHES which were occupied in force. The attack by the 3rd Division on our Right was also unsuccessful, and by night-time our Infantry occupied their original line, with the exception of our extreme right which was-that occupied that portion of ARROW TRENCH to the North of BIT LANE.	Ands. And. And. And. And.
	14th		A CHINESE Attack was made on the enemy, and an organised bombardment of his positions was carried out. The Division on our left co-operated with enfilade Machine Gun fire. The barrage came down simultaneously and was reported upon satisfactorily. No movement however, was reported as being seen as a result. Up to 9 p.m. occasional rounds were fired on PELVES-HAMBLAIN Road as far east to the cross-roads at I.28 a.5.9. (This road has been fired on in this manner for several nights and has caused the enemy to use a track running parallel to this road and about 150 yards south of it. At 9 p.m. all Batteries fired 5 rounds Gun-fire along this track. Registration and light Bombardment of C RTRIDGE & GUN TRENCHES was carried out.	And. And. And.

Army Form C. 2118.

WAR DIARY
or
INTELLIGENCE SUMMARY

(Erase heading not required.)

162nd Brigade. R.F.A.

MAY -1917 (Cont'd).

Place	Date	Hour	Summary of Events and Information	Remarks and references to Appendices
	16th		About 3.0 a.m. the enemy attacked and captured the CEMETERY and CHEMICAL WORKS (ROEUX). By 7.30 a.m. we re-captured the CEMETERY & CHEMICAL WORKS. At 9.50 a.m. the enemy counter-attacked on the CHEMICAL WORKS but evidently failed, as at 10.7 a.m. our men were seen advancing N.E. from the CHEMICAL WORKS owing to a very thick Hostile barrage. (or the need to place) Fighting continued throughout the day.	
	19th		An attack was carried out to capture DEVIL'S TRENCH. As soon as our Artillery barrage open the enemy opened very heavy concentrated Machine Gun fire - he also put down an effective Artillery barrage within 30 seconds after ours. A footing was gained in the part of TOOL TRENCH which was still in the enemy's hands, but strong bombing attacks were made against both flanks and our Troops were forced to withdraw. The enemy's fire rendered an advance impossible. Result - line remains unchanged.	
	30/31st		At 11.30 p.m. a small enterprise was attempted with the object of capturing HOOK TRENCH and the portion of TOOL TRENCH held by the enemy. Our Troops were evidently seen leaving there Trenches, and this enabled the enemy to inflict casualties with Artillery and M.G. fire. In spite of this and in spite of the Mud and water caused by the thunder-storm in the afternoon, the attacking troops reached their objective, but owing to casualties were not strong enough to deal with the garrison of the trench and were driven back by a counter-attack. Between O.2.b.3.4. and O.2.d.3.8. a party of the Manchester Regt: established itself in HOOK TRENCH and held on until about noon 31st. when it was overcome by the superior force of the enemy. We established a new post at about I.25 d.55.55.	

Army Form C. 2118.

WAR DIARY
or
INTELLIGENCE SUMMARY

162nd Brigade. R.F.A.

(Erase heading not required.)

MAY-1917 (Contd.)

Place	Date	Hour	Summary of Events and Information	Remarks and references to Appendices
			CASUALTIES.	

Battle Casualties.
(Killed in Action   1 Officer 3 Other ranks
(Died of Wounds.   1 Officer.
(Wounded & Evacuated.   16 Other ranks.
(Wounded (at duty.)   1 Officer 4 other ranks.

Sick and evacuated 31 Other ranks.
Discharged from Hospital 6 Other ranks.
Posted to Brigade.   70 other ranks.
Posted away from Brigade. 22 Other ranks.

OFFICER CASUALTIES.

Captain E.R.Heape   Killed in action 16.5.17.
2nd Lieut ..R.Tucker   wounded "   (16.5.17.
                                                          Died   (17±5.17.
Lieut.Col. C.M.Harris, D.S.O.) Admitted to Hospital
     O.C., Brigade.   17.5.17.
Major W.P. Colfox Commanded Brigade from 18.5.17. to 23.5.17.
Lieut.E.M.Conolly, posted to Command Brigade 24.5.17.
     Col.

Capt.A.M.I.Body   ) Awarded MILITARY CROSS
2nd Lieut.J.B.Barnes   ) vide. Corps R.O.2122 D/12.5.17.
2nd Lieut.W.E.Harrison.) (VIth Corps.)

[signature] Lieut.Colonel.R.F.A.
               Commanding 162nd Brigade.R.F.A.

PROMOTIONS - OFFICERS.
/Capt.I.C.Hill promoted a/Major.
2nd Lieut.J.H.Barnes promoted A/Capt.
2nd Lieut.J.V.Macartney Filgate promoted a/Capt.
vide 33rd D.A.H.Q. No.247 D/21.5.17.
with effect from that date.

WAR DIARY
of
INTELLIGENCE SUMMARY

162nd Brigade R.F.A.,

JUNE 1917.

Instructions regarding War Diaries and Intelligence Summaries are contained in F.S. Regs., Part II. and the Staff Manual respectively. Title Pages will be prepared in manuscript.

(Erase heading not required.)

Summary of Events and Information

Place	Date	Hour	Summary of Events and Information
	3rd	8 p.m.,	Brigade still in action south of FEUCHY. The Brigade co-operated with the 9th Division (north of the River SCARPE) in a Chinese attack at 8.0 p.m., and again at 7.30 a.m., on the 4th.
	5/6th		During the night 5/6th June, the Division on our left (9th Div) carried out a successful attack, our troops reaching their objectives and establishing themselves along the front of the ground gained. An isolated nest of Germans who held on was afterwards cleaned out. The line now held comprises CUPID, CURLY, and CH RLIE trenches continuously. CUTHBERT, and CUD Trenches are also reported to be held by us. A new trench runs from I.14.a.5.4 to I.14.a.6.0 and a new communication trench from CURSE to CHARLIE trenches. Prisoners reported number 5 Officers and 173 Other Ranks. The Brigade assisted by putting up - thickening barrage.
	13th		At 7.20 a.m., two battalions of our right Division attacked HOOK and LONG Trenches. The attack was carried out as a surprise without an artillery barrage, and was completely successful, our objectives having been gained by 7.27 a.m., and an advanced post established at the MOUND at about the same time. Owing to the dash with which the attack was made, the enemy was taken completely by surprise and offered little resistance. Our new line now runs from MITRE COPSE along LONG trench to about O.2.b.5.2. thence along original front line. A light barrage of 77 m.m was put down by the enemy one minute after ZERO. Machine gun fire opened from the BOIS DES AUBEPINES and the BOIS DU VERT at 7.30 a.m., The number of prisoners captured was 3 Officers and 172 Other ranks (including 1 Officer and 23 Other ranks wounded).

WAR DIARY
or
INTELLIGENCE SUMMARY

(Erase heading not required.)

162nd Brigade R.F.A.,

JUNE, 1917.

Instructions regarding War Diaries and Intelligence
Summaries are contained in F. S. Regs., Part II.
and the Staff Manual respectively. Title Pages
will be prepared in manuscript.

Place	Date	Hour	Summary of Events and Information
	14th		At 7.15 a.m., an attack was made, resulting in the capture of INFANTRY HILL. Our troops also dug in just behind and parallel to LONG Trench and then through southern of TWIN COPSES. Strong posts were established on the MOUND about I.5.c.1.7 and then in a line south to L of LONG. 170 prisoners were taken. At 5.40 p.m., the enemy counter-attacked, but were dispersed by our artillery fire.
	16th		At 2.15 a.m., the enemy heavily counter-attacked INFANTRY HILL supported by an intense artillery bombardment. Attacking strength about 700 strong in mixed companies. 2 southern posts in front of LONG Trench were relinquished otherwise we maintained our gains of the 14th. 5 Officers and 175 Other ranks of the enemy were captured.
	17th		At 12.30 a.m., the enemy put down a heavy barrage on INFANTRY Hill and at 2.30 a.m., made a strong attack on LONG and HOOK Trenches. He succeeded in capturing the northern part of LONG trench, but south of GREEN LINE it remains in our possession.
	20th		At 5.0 p.m., the Brigade moved out of action and stayed the night at wagon lines north of ARRAS.
	21st		Brigade marched to new wagon lines between BOUELLES and HABLINCOURT. Batteries moved into action under command of the 82nd, 83rd, and 250th Brigade Groups. Headquarters remained out of action.
	23/24th		"A" & "B" Batteries came under command of 251st Bde Group. "C" & "D" Batteries under 250th Bde Group.

162nd Brigade R.F.A.,

WAR DIARY
or
INTELLIGENCE SUMMARY
(*Erase heading not required.*)

Instructions regarding War Diaries and Intelligence Summaries are contained in F.S. Regs., Part II. and the Staff Manual respectively. Title Pages will be prepared in manuscript.

JUNE, 1917.

Place	Date	Hour	Summary of Events and Information
	25th		The zones allotted to the batteries were roughly speaking West of FONTAINES LES CROISALLES. For the first time for some months we were in touch with our Infantry (53rd) although actually shooting over a sector immediately north of that part of the HINDENBURG LINE garrisoned by the 98th and 19th Infantry Brigades. At 12.30 a.m., on the 25th we co-operated in an attack made by the 5th E.Yorks on YORK, BUSH, and WOOD Trenches and succeeded in obtaining practically the whole of our objectives, and together with 30 prisoners, with the exception of the Cross Roads U.1.d.7.9. Two counter-attacks were repelled but part of the ground gained was evacuated owing to hostile destructive fire demolishing the newly gained trenches. At other times our fire was directed (chiefly at night) on hostile tracks and approaches between FONTAINES and CHERISY, about 600 rounds being fired every 24 hours. Hostile counter battery work was in evidence but no casualties were sustained although "A" Battery position at T.4.d.7.8 was much damaged on 22nd and 24th. The Brigade's reputation for straight shooting was well maintained. On the 30th the position of the batteries was as follows:- "A" Battery T.4.d.7.8. "D" Battery N.34.c.9.7 "B" Battery N.34.d.8.0., H.Q. at S.23.b.4.5. "C" Battery N.28.b.3.2., All waggon lines at S.23.b. & S.17.d. ------o0o------

WAR DIARY
INTELLIGENCE SUMMARY

162nd Brigade R.F.A., JUNE 1917.

(Erase heading not required.)

Instructions regarding War Diaries and Intelligence Summaries are contained in F.S. Regs., Part II. and the Staff Manual respectively. Title Pages will be prepared in manuscript.

Place	Date	Hour	Summary of Events and Information
			CASUALTIES.
			Officers.
			Lieut-Col O.A.Harris, D.S.O., to England, sick and struck off Strength 2-6-17.
			2nd Lieut C.W.Almack to 16th Bde R.H.A., 2-6-17.
			2nd Lieut H.R.Edwards Joined 3-6-17.
			Major C.G.H.Walker, Joined 6-6-17.
			2nd Lieut G.T.S.Clarke Joined 6-6-17.
			2nd Lieut V.A.Barton Joined 14-6-17.
			2nd Lieut E.J.H.Kitchen Joined 14-6-17.
			2nd Lieut V.W.Cunis Joined 15-6-17. (from 33rd D.A.C).
			2nd Lieut F.C.Rose To 33rd D.A.C., 15-6-17.
			2nd Lieut S.T.G.Donovan Joined 22-6-17.
			Battle Casualties - Nil.
			Men :-
			Admitted to Hospital - 23.
			Discharged from Hospital - 12.
			Posted to Brigade - 58.
			Posted away from Brigade - 12.
			Battle Casualties - 1 Wounded.
			2 Wounded (Remained at duty).

[signed] Lieut-Col R.F.A.,
Commanding 162nd Brigade, R.F.A.,

Original to D.A.G., G.H.Q., via 33rd Div. Arty.
Duplicate to O i/c R.H. & R.F.A. Records, Woolwich Dockyard, S.E.,

162nd Brigade R.F.A., JULY 1917.

WAR DIARY
or
INTELLIGENCE SUMMARY

(Erase heading not required.)

Place	Date	Hour	Summary of Events and Information
	1st		Batteries still in action. "C" Battery in Héninel., "A", "B", & "D" Batteries west of the HINDENBURG LINE and 9e opposite Chérisy.
	Night 11/12th		Batteries pulled out of action to their wagon lines between BOYELLES and HAMELINCOURT.
	12th - 23rd		From the 12th to the 23rd the Brigade went into Training. All guns were sent to the I.O.M., for overhaul. Brigade equipment which had become depleted owing to the inevitable wear and tear sustained during a prolonged period in action was made up to Mobilisation Strength. On 2d day of the eleven was devoted to a Divisional Artillery Horse show and another to sports. On the 13th Advance parties from the Brigade entrained from BEAUMETZ and proceeded to 1st Division Headquarters at COXYDE BAINS on the Belgian coast.
	23rd		The Brigade marched from wagon lines to AUTHIEULE (About 2 miles from DOULLENS), where they were billetted for the night.
	24th		From noon to 6.0 p.m., batteries entrained at AUTHIEULE, whilst Headquarters marched independantly to DOULLENS SOUTH Station where they entrained.
	25th		Batteries and Headquarters detrained at DUNKERQUE and marched to GHYVELDE, a village about 1 mile south of the DUNKERQUE - NIEUPORT Canal and 2 miles from the Belgian Frontier. Here the Brigade encamped and wagon lines were established.
	26th		Forward wagon lines established at COXYDE BAINS.
	28th		Batteries calibrated their guns, firing from the beach near COXYDE into the sea.

WAR DIARY or INTELLIGENCE SUMMARY

162nd Brigade R.F.A.,

JULY 1917.

Place	Date	Hour	Summary of Events and Information
	28th		Headquarters, "A", "B", & "C" Batteries moved into action. Considerable difficulty was experienced owing to the enemy shelling the neighbourhood with shell gas during the night. Respirators were worn for 2½ hours. No casualties sustained.
	30th		"D" Battery moved into action. Positions in action were as follows :- Headquarters in the West Sand Dunes about 700 yards south of GROENENDYK PLAGE. "A" Battery about 200 yards and "B" Battery about 100 yards in rear of Headquarters. "C" & "D" Batteries in advance of Headquarters and south of the GROENENDYK PLAGE - NIEUPORT BAINS Road. "C" Battery in the West Dunes, "D" Battery in the East Dunes, about 300 yards and 150 yards respectively from the Coast. The front on which the Brigade fired was held by 66th Division Infantry, and was known as the NIEUPORT BAINS Sector, extending from the Coast along the south side of the YSER along NEW TRENCH to BARNES BRIDGE. The Sector was held by one Infantry Brigade with 2 Battalions in the line. Artillery support consisted of 33rd & 66th Divisional Artilleries and 3 Army Field Artillery Brigades formed into 5 Groups under the Command of Brigadier General D.B.STEWART, D.S.O., C.R.A., 66th Division (XV Corps, 4th Army). 162nd Brigade R.F.A., formed "E" Group. The Brigade used an O.P., known as Dune 18 O.P., situated about 500 yards South West of NIEUPORT BAINS. "E" Group assisted in a dummy barrage on PUNCH TRENCH.
	31st		Wagon Lines moved from the GHYVELDE area to KURSAAL LA PANNE.

WAR DIARY or INTELLIGENCE SUMMARY

162nd Brigade R.F.A.,   JULY 1917.

(Erase heading not required.)

Instructions regarding War Diaries and Intelligence Summaries are contained in F.S. Regs., Part II. and the Staff Manual respectively. Title Pages will be prepared in manuscript.

Place	Date	Hour	Summary of Events and Information
			C A S U A L T I E S.
			Officers:-
			2nd Lieut W.E.Harrison, proceeded to Army Headquarters 21-7-17 to report for duty (To command a Trench Mortar Battery).
			2nd Lieut G.Bartholomew Admitted to Hospital sick 20-7-17.
			Men :-
			Wounded - 6 (including 1 remaining at duty).
			Sick - Admitted to Hospital 18.
			Discharged from Hospital to duty 10.
			Posted to Brigade 15.
			Posted from Brigade 2.
			[signature]
			Lieut-Colonel R.F.A.,
			Commanding 162nd Brigade R.F.A.,
			1-8-1917.

Army Form C. 2118.

162nd Brigade R.G.A.

WAR DIARY
~~INTELLIGENCE SUMMARY~~
(Erase heading not required.)

August 1917.

Place	Date	Hour	Summary of Events and Information	Remarks and references to Appendices
	1st		Brigade still in action in positions as occupied 29th July 1917.	
	1–27th		This period was spent in general harassing fire destructive fire (i.e, shell observation on hostile batteries, bombardments in co-operation with the operation etc.).	
	24th		We co-operated in an infantry enterprise made by 1st Division (who were Battalion infantry at the time) which resulted in the capture of a German post on the neighbourhood of LOMBARTZYDE. A machine gun & 7 prisoners were annexed.	
	23rd		Headquarters moved into a house in NIEUPORT BAINS, the roof of which afforded an excellent O.P.	
	27th		Batteries and Headquarters pulled out of action to huts lines near ST. IDESBALDE.	

W. Shuter
Major R.G.A.
Commanding 162nd Brigade R.G.A.

162nd Brigade R.F.A.

WAR DIARY
or
INTELLIGENCE SUMMARY

Army Form C. 2118.

August 1917.

Place	Date	Hour	Summary of Events and Information	Remarks and references to Appendices
			Casualties:-	
			Officers:- Lieut-Col. E.M. Connelly to 11th Division Hd.Qrs. Major M.A. Stuart, M.C., temporarily posted from 156th Brigade R.F.A. to command 162nd Brigade R.F.A. 30th. Lieut. N.K. Brooks posted to Balloon Section R.F.C., 9th. Lieut. G. Bartholomew to England sick, struck off 18th. Major C.H.G. Walker wounded 25th (remained at duty).	
			Men:- Died of wounds - 2. Wounded & evacuated 8. Wounded & remained at duty. 10. T. Shellshock - 146 (21 wounded). Discharge from hospital to Unit - 11. Posted Away - 5. Posted to Brigade - 6.	

Army Form C. 2118.

162nd BRIGADE R.F.A.,

WAR DIARY
or
INTELLIGENCE SUMMARY
(Erase heading not required.)

September 1917.

Instructions regarding War Diaries and Intelligence Summaries are contained in F. S. Regs., Part II. and the Staff Manual respectively. Title Pages will be prepared in manuscript.

Place	Date	Hour	Summary of Events and Information	Remarks and references to Appendices
	1st		Brigade still at wagon lines near ST. IDESBALDE. Orders received to move to 2nd Army area starting 2nd inst.,	
	2nd		Brigade marched to UXEM area via ADINKERKE and GHYVELDE.	
	3rd		Brigade marched to WORMHOUDT - ZERMEZEELE area via REXPOEDE.	
	4th		Brigade marched to RENINGHELST area via CASSEL, STEENVOORDE, and ABEELE. Wagon Lines established at ALBERTA CAMP about 700 yards S.W. of RENINGHELST.	
	5th to 13th		Batteries send up parties, and with the help of Trench Mortar personnel, built their respective battery positions and also 2 positions for the 23rd Div. Arty.	
	Night 13/14		"A", "B", & "C" Batteries moved into action on the eastern side of ZILLEBEKE about 1½ miles S.E. of YPRES.	
	Night 14/15		"D" Battery moved into action in the same area. The front covered was from the S.W edge of the POLYGONE DE ZONNEBEKE southward about 700 yards. "C" Battery were in RIGHT GROUP, under the command of Lieut-Col E.A.B.Butler, 156th Brigade R.F.A. ; the other batteries were in LEFT GROUP, under the command of Lieut-Col GROVES, 103rd Brigade R.F.A., 23rd Div. Arty.	
	15th		Forward wagon lines established near the eastern side of DICKEBUSCH under the charge of 2nd Lieut J.H.K.Rayson. The horses kept here were used for packing ammunition from the forward dumps up to the battery positions.	

Army Form C. 2118.

WAR DIARY
or
INTELLIGENCE SUMMARY

162nd BRIGADE, R.F.A.,

(Erase heading not required.)

Instructions regarding War Diaries and Intelligence Summaries are contained in F. S. Regs., Part II. and the Staff Manual respectively. Title Pages will be prepared in manuscript.

Place	Date	Hour	Summary of Events and Information	Remarks and references to Appendices
	20th		The batteries took part in an attack made on 2nd and 5th Army fronts, covering the 23rd Division. The 2nd Australian Division were on our left and the 41st Division on our right. All objectives were ultimately gained after heavy and severe fighting.	
	Night 20/21		Forward wagon lines shelled out and moved to the other side of the road by DICKEBUSCH church.	
	23rd		"C" Battery shelled out. Battery position was moved 300 yards to a left flank.	
	25th		Enemy heavily counter attacked on our Infantry (33rd Division) who had just come into the line but all ground was maintained. Letter of congratulation from the Commander-in-Chief attached. Rear wagon lines moved forward to about 1000 yards S.E., or DICKEBUSCH.	
	26th		Attack was made on a large scale on the 2nd Army front. Our Batteries covered our own infantry. The 5th Australian Division was on our left and the 39th Division on our right. After very severe fighting all objectives were eventually gained.	
	27th		"B" Battery withdrew to their wagon lines. B/162 took over from them. In the line.	
	28th		Headquarters moved forward and took over command of LEFT GROUP from 103rd Brigade R.F.A., at DUMMY HOUSE. The batteries in the Group were A/162, D/162, B/103, B/103, C/103, D/103, the letter four being batteries of the 23rd Divisional Artillery. The front covered was from a point 500 yards west of the S.E. corner of the POLYGON DE ZONNEBEKE to a point 700 yards south of CAMERON HOUSE. The front covered by the whole Div. Arty extended from GHELUVELT-ZONNEBEKE Road to about 1500 yards north.	

Casualties - September 1917.

Officers -

- 6th Lieut-Col E.J.Skinner, D.S.O., posted from 49th D.A., to Command Brigade.
- 6th 2nd Lieut R.C.Norton, admitted to hospital sick.
- 19th Major W.P.Colfox.   )
  - 2nd Lieut R.C.Odhams.   ) Wounded in Action.
  - 2nd Lieut E.J.H.Kitchen.   )
- 22nd 2nd Lieut J.G.J.Chapman, Wounded in Action.
- 21st 2nd Lieut V.A.Barton, Killed in Action.
- 23rd 2nd Lieut W.Hannaford, posted to Brigade.
- 25th 2nd Lieut E.T.G.Donovan, Wounded (Gas).
- 26th Major C.H.G.Walker, admitted to hospital suffering from effects of Gas Poisoning.
  - 2nd Lieut V.W.Cunis, Wounded in action.
- 27th 2nd Lieut A.C.Mousley, posted to Brigade.
  - 2nd Lieut H.R.Edwards, wounded in action.
- 28th Capt F.L.Lee. posted to command D/162 from D/156 R.F.A.,
- 6th Capt E.G.Lutyens posted away to 4th Div. Arty.
- 9th 2nd Lieut H.A.Thompson, wounded at duty.

Men.

Killed in action - 17.

Died of wounds - 3.

Wounded and evacuated - 53. (including 10 gas casualties).

Wounded at Duty. - 9.

Admitted to hospital sick - 31. (15 evacuated, 8 rejoined).

Posted to Brigade - 59.

Posted away from Brigade - 9.

E.J. Skinner

Lieut-Col R.F.A.,
Commanding 162nd Brigade R.F.A.,

Army Form C. 2118.

WAR DIARY
or
INTELLIGENCE-SUMMARY.
(Erase heading not required.)

162nd Brigade R.F.A.,

OCTOBER 1917.

Vol 23

Place	Date	Hour	Summary of Events and Information	Remarks and references to Appendices
	1st.		"A", "C", & "D" Batteries still in action East of ZILLEBEKE. "B" Battery still at wagon lines 1000 yds S.E. of DICKEBUSCH. Headquarters moved from JONNY HOUSE to BEDFORD HOUSE, still retaining command of left Group.	
	3rd.		119th & 120th Batteries of 5th Div. Arty joined left Group.	
	4th.		Left Group Artillery covered 5th Div. Infantry in an attack made on Army front. The going was heavy but after severe fighting all objectives were gained. A counter attack was broken up by our Artillery fire. The infantry agreed that the barrage throughout was excellent.	
	7th.		Groups under 5th Div. Arty reformed. We became No. 3 Group and lost the 119th and 120th Batteries. B/162 came back into action, taking over from B/242 and joining No. 2 Group.	
	9th.		5th Div. Infantry covered by Groups of 5th Div. Arty attacked POLDERHOEK CHATEAU. Owing to the bad state of the ground no advance was made on "C" Group front but a little further north all objectives were gained.	
	13th.		Brigade Headquarters relieved/203rd Brigade Headquarters 23rd Division. Bde H.Q. moved to LA CLYTTE. Personnel of D/162 withdrawn to Wagon lines for short rest.	
	17th.		Personnel of D/162 returned into action.	
	18th.		Personnel of A/162 and C/162 withdrawn to Wagon lines for short rest.	
	23rd.		Personnel of A/162 returned into action. Personnel of C/162 remained at wagon lines, having had 94 casualties	

Army Form C. 2118.

WAR DIARY
or
INTELLIGENCE SUMMARY.

162nd Brigade R.F.A.,

(Erase heading not required.)

OCTOBER 1917.

Instructions regarding War Diaries and Intelligence Summaries are contained in F. S. Regs., Part II. and the Staff Manual respectively. Title pages will be prepared in manuscript.

Place	Date	Hour	Summary of Events and Information	Remarks and references to Appendices
	24th		during their stay in action were not in a position to go back into action with A/162 on 23rd.	
	26th		Bde H.Q., relieved 103rd Bde H.Q., at BEDFORD HOUSE, and took over command of "C" Group, 7th D.A., at 10.0 a.m. "C" Group consisting of A/162, B/162, D/162, B/156, 46th, 47th & 112th Australian Batteries. The frontcovered by "C" Group was changed from north of GHELUVELT to just south of it which gave a shorter range for the batteries. The Infantry now covered were the 20th Infantry Brigade, 7th Division. "C" Group participated in a barrage beneath which the 2nd Border Regiment and 2nd Devon Regt., both of 7th Division attacked GHELUVELT and the high ground on which the village stood. After heavy fighting the Infantry were forced to return to very nearly their starting point owing to the bad state of the ground and machine gun fire from one or two strong points.	
	24th		D/162 moved their battery position about 800 yards north.	
	27th		47th Aus. Battery personnel removed to their wagon lines.	
	29th		Groups came under the tactical command of 39th Div. Arty who had taken over from 7th Div. Arty. Groups reformed. "C" Group retained its original batteries and had in addition D/156 whose position was near SANCTUARY WOOD, and who were formerly in "B" Group.	
	31st		D/155 came out of action and proceeded to their wagon lines.	

Casualties - October 1917.

Officers -

2nd Lieut D.Fitch.   Killed in action.
2nd Lieut G.F.Dean.   Killed in action.
Major F.L.Lee.   Wounded at Duty.
2nd Lieut H.J.Escott.   Wounded at Duty.
Major L.C.Hill.   Wounded (Gas) at Duty.

2nd Lieut W.H.Topliss-Green   Admitted to Hospital sick.
Capt. F.H.Warr, M.C.,   Admitted to Hospital sick.

2nd Lieut R.C.Norton.   Rejoined from Hospital.

Men. -

Killed in Action.   -   16.

Died of Wounds   -   6.7 (including 1 from effects of Gas).

Wounded.   -   39.

Wounded at Duty   -   15.

Gassed.   -   68.

Gassed at Duty   -   8.   (4 subsequently admitted to Hospital)

Missing.   -   1.

Admitted to Hospital   -   33.   (8 evacuated).

Discharged from Hospital to Duty   -   4.

Posted to Brigade   -   171.

Posted away from Brigade   -   3.

Lieut-Colonel R.F.A
Commanding 162nd Brigade R.F.A.,

5th Division No. G.S.157.

C. R. A. 5th Division.
C. R. A. 23rd —"—
C. R. A. 33rd —"—
242nd Army F.A. Brigade.
O.C. Right Double Group. H.A.

G.O.C. 5th Division wishes to thank the Artillery for their admirable work on October 4th. All reports from the Infantry agree that the barrage was excellent.

The G.O.C., 5th Division would like the gunners to know that the Infantry thoroughly realize the immense amount of work and endurance that is necessary to keep up the artillery fire that is asked for.

5th Division.   sd. G.W. RUPTON HALL,   Lieut. Colonel.
6th Oct. 1917.   General Staff.

-2-

5th Divisional Artillery No. AXA/2003/15.

O.C. Right Group.
    Centre Group.
    Left Group.

For information.

Headquarters.   Major R.A.
R.A. 5th Divn.
7th Oct. 1917.   Brigade Major, R.A. 5th Division.

AA.
33rd Div'l Art.

Herewith 2nd Sheet of War Diary.
the Diary is not continued further than the
12/4/17 because the Bde was at ALQUINES
from that date until the end of the month.

Lovitt
11/31/7   for O.C 1/2 Bde RFA   Capt & Adjt RFA

162nd Brigade R.F.A., WAR DIARY or INTELLIGENCE SUMMARY

Army Form C. 2118.

162 Bde R.F.A. WO 2/4

NOVEMBER 1917.

(Erase heading not required.)

Place	Date	Hour	Summary of Events and Information	Remarks and references to Appendices
	1st.		Brigade still in action in positions as detailed in "October War Diary.	
	3rd.		Brigade withdrew from action and proceeded to Wagon Lines S.E., of PICKEBUSCH. Headquarters established at WESTOUTRE.	
			During the period the Brigade was in action on the YPRES Front (i.e., from 13-9-17 to 3-11-17 – 51 days) 315 battle casualties were sustained including 136 Gas Casualties.	
	5th.		Brigade proceeded to VIII Corps training area via HAZEBROUCK, CAILLON CAPPEL, STAPLE.	
			Headquarters were billetted in EAMINGHOVE.	
			"A" Battery in ZUYTPEENE) south
			"B" Battery in OXELAERE) of
			"C" Battery in ZUYTPEENE) CASSEL.
			"D" Battery in TROIS ROIS)
	12th.		Brigade proceeded to neighbourhood of BOUVELINGHEM via ARQUES, WIZERNES, SECQUES, A COUIN.	
			Headquarters were billetted in AQUINES.	
			"A" & "B" Batteries in AQUINES.	
			"C" Battery in LE BUISSON.	
			"D" Battery in HAUTE PLAQUE.	
				P.T.O.,

Army Form C. 2118.

General
Sept 25

WAR DIARY
or
INTELLIGENCE SUMMARY.
(Erase heading not required.)

December 1917.   162nd Bde R.F.A.

P.16.

Place	Date	Hour	Summary of Events and Information	Remarks and references to Appendices
	1st		Brigade still at rest at ALQUINES — HAUTE PLANQUE — LE BUISSON. Orders received for the Brigade to go into action forthwith.	
	2nd		Brigade marched to ZERMEZEELE area & billeted overnight. Orders received that the Bde were to relieve 266 A.F.A. Bde on 3rd inst Bde., Bde M.Gr. to take over Mhro. No. 2 Group. (266 A.F.A. Bde Mhro.) 33rd A.A. Group.	
	3rd	7.30am	Personnel of Gun Section per Battery proceeded by lorries from ZERMEZEELE Church to forward area, where they were met by guides of 26 A.F.A. Bde & conducted to Battery Positions. Remainder of Bde marched from ZERMEZEELE to Wagon lines about 3 mile West of YPRES. (Remaining Battery Sections of the Mhro. relieved corresponding Sections of Bde Mhro of 266 A.F.A. Bde. Command passed at 2 p.m.	
	4th		The Bde H.A. Group (consisting of 3 Groups — in Right, Left & Intermediate) covered the PASSCHENDAELE RIDGE — CREST FARM — MEETCHEELE line. We carried our own infantry. (i.e., 33rd Div.). Batts in No. 2 Group, Commanded by Lieut-Col. L.T. SKINNER D.S.O., were A, B & C/162. D/162 was in No. 1 Group Commanded by Lieut-Col. G.A. Burles, 156th Bde/F.A.	

Army Form C. 2118.

Original

WAR DIARY
INTELLIGENCE SUMMARY.

December — 1917.   162nd Bde R.F.A.

(Erase heading not required.)

Instructions regarding War Diaries and Intelligence Summaries are contained in F. S. Regs., Part II. and the Staff Manual respectively. Title pages will be prepared in manuscript.

Place	Date	Hour	Summary of Events and Information	Remarks and references to Appendices
	7th		Bde. HQrs withdrawn from Order to Wagon Lines after having handed over command of No.2. Group to Lieut-Col LORD. A.E. BROWNE, 186th Bde. A.R. & Offr came under command of No.1. Group.	
	10th & 20th		Batteries withdrawn to Wagon Line.	
	23rd		Bde. marched to Reserve Div. Art. Waggon Lines about 1 mile S.E. of POPERINGHE. During this time the unit it moved the Bde personnel in the construction of Horse Standings & Stables with a view to making a permanent camp.	
	30th		Orders received that the positions for Bde of Field Art to cover the Army Defence Zone to be prepared immediately for occupation. 162 Bde to be responsible for one of these positions. Area allotted was just west of POTIJZE CHATEAU. Work was commenced at once.	P.T.O.

WAR DIARY / INTELLIGENCE SUMMARY

162 Brigade R.F.A.
December 1917.

Army Form C. 2118.
Original

Casualties — Officers —

- 4th. 2/Lt. J.W. Chambers joined.
- 7th. 2/Lt. R. Vickers. Wounded. (Died 10/12/17).
- 9th. 2/Lt. W.A. Runton struck off. (Medical Board in England).
- 10th. 2/Lt. A. Hannaford Wounded.
- 10th. Lieut. E.E. Gibbon joined.
- 23rd. Lieut. A.G. Perkins joined.
- 26th. 2/Lt. E. Bartholomew joined.
- 27th. Lieut. J.A.K. Pearson struck off. (Medical Board in England).
- 29th. 2/Lt. S.H. Sedgewick James.

Men — Killed 6.
Wounded 20.
Admitted to Hospital 33 (via evacuation).
Discharged from Hospital to duty 15.
Posted to Bde. 61.
Posted away from Bde. 2.

2/1/1918.

[signature]
for O/C 162 Bde. R.F.A. Cdr. + Adj 162th.

Copy

CASUALTIES.

Officers. -

5-11-17. 2nd Lieut L.M.Howard (Wounded - Gas).
8-11-17. 2nd Lieut W.D.Davies posted to 2nd D.A.,
21-11-17. Major W.G.Pringle, M.C., to England (War Office Instructions).

Men. -

Wounded 4.

Wounded at Duty 1.

Gassed. 8.

Gassed at duty 1.

Admitted to Hospital 30 (8 evacuated).

Discharged from Hospital to duty 4.

Posted to Brigade 61.

Posted away from Brigade 10.

E.J. Skinner
Lieut-Col R.F.A.,
Commanding 162nd Brigade R.F.A.,

5-12-17.

162nd Brigade R.F.A. WAR DIARY

INTELLIGENCE SUMMARY

JANUARY. 1918.

Place	Date	Hour	Summary of Events and Information	Remarks and references to Appendices
	1st		Brigade still in reserve 2 miles S.E. of POPERINGHE.	
	1st to 6th		Time passed was spent by the batteries in the construction of suitable battery positions in front of POTIJZE Chateau 1½ miles N.E. of YPRES.	
	7th		One section per battery moved into action in positions in the vicinity of ABRAHAM HEIGHTS, relieving corresponding sections of 251 Bde. R.F.A. 50th D.A.	
	8th		Remaining Battery positions. Sections moved into action. Headquarters took over command of No. 2. Group. HQrs situated in a "pill-box" just off the main YPRES – ZONNEBEKE Road in front of FREZENBURG. The Brigade was temporarily commanded by Major N.G.M. JERVIS in the absence of Lieut-Col E.J. SKINNER, D.S.O., who commanded the 2nd D.A. Group. We relieved 33rd Division Infantry who held PASSCHENDAELE VILLAGE.	
	9th		"B", "C" + "D" Batteries Wagon lines Headquarters Wagon Lines took over 50th D.A. Wagon lines 1 mile S.E of VLAMERTINGHE. A/162 took over their old Wagon lines just off the main POPERINGHE – YPRES Rd about 1 mile West of YPRES.	

162nd Brigade R.F.A. WAR DIARY

Army Form C. 2118.

Instructions regarding War Diaries and Intelligence Summaries are contained in F. S. Regs., Part II. and the Staff Manual respectively. Title pages will be prepared in manuscript.

INTELLIGENCE SUMMARY.

JANUARY 1918.

(Erase heading not required.)

Place	Date	Hour	Summary of Events and Information	Remarks and references to Appendices
	29th		One Section per battery relieved by corresponding Section of 251 R.F.A. Personnel of relieved Sections proceeded to Wagon Lines.	
	30th		Remaining Sections of above relieved. Gun Line personnel proceeded to Junior & OUDEZEELE, the firing Battery Wagon Lines were kept under fire by Wagon Lines near VLAMERTINGHE.	
	31st		R.F. left OUDEZEELE & marched to the LE BAS & BERGUES area.	

(Signed) J. W. [illegible]
Lieut. Col. R.F.A.
Commanding 162 R.F.A. Bde.

Army Form C. 2118.

162nd Brigade.

WAR DIARY
or
INTELLIGENCE SUMMARY.

JANUARY. 1918. *(Erase heading not required.)*

Place	Date	Hour	Summary of Events and Information	Remarks and references to Appendices
			Casualties:-	
			Officers:- 2/Lt. C.A. Squires. ⎱ 9-1-18.	
			2/Lt. H.J. Chalmont. ⎰ 22-1-18.	
			2/Lt. W.H. Kerr. ⎱ 23-1-18. Joined	
			2/Lt. C.R. Moine. ⎰ 27-1-18.	
			2/Lt. L.R. Yoher. ⎱ 27-1-18.	
			Major A. Nethersole. ⎰ 11-1-18.	
			2/Lt. I.P. McNall. Wounded Evacuated 9-1-18.	
			Men:- Died of Wounds. 1.	
			Wounded. 6.	
			Admitted to Hospital 30. (16 evacuated).	
			Discharged from Hospital to Duty. 3.	
			Posted to Brigade. 77.	
			Posted from Bde. 1.	

Army Form C. 2118.

162ND BRIGADE,
ROYAL
FIELD ARTILLERY.

WAR DIARY
—of—
INTELLIGENCE SUMMARY.

(Erase heading not required.)

February 1918.

Place	Date	Hour	Summary of Events and Information	Remarks and references to Appendices
	1st		The Brigade left the LE BAS — SERQUES area & marched to Rear Area — "A" & "B" Batteries & HQrs were at MERCK ST LIEVIN. "C" Battery was at FAUQUEMBERGUES. "D" Battery was at BOUT DE LA VILLE.	
	2nd		Bde HQrs moved from MERCK-ST-LIEVIN to FAUQUEMBERGUES.	
	3rd to 19th		This period was spent in Rest & Training. Mornings were devoted to Gun Drill, Signalling, Driving Drill etc.; Afternoons to Recreational Training, and Evenings to Lectures. Sports (Football, Boxing, Tug-of-War) were encouraged throughout the Div.l Artillery. Whenever practicable Bde horses were taken to throughfares overhaul. British Equipment, Men's clothing & vehicles were re-painted. Gunner & howitzer camouflage. On 13th Orders were received that the Div. Artillery would relieve 50th Div.l Artillery on the line on 22nd & 23rd... On 14th & 15th all 18pdr guns were calibrated by a Sound Ranging Section at a range near PIERRES WITH Guns & 10/15 firing from at ST MARTIN-AU-LAERT. On 17th & 18th "A" & "B" Batteries carried out scheme set by B.R.A. 1st Army. (S.W.S. 130) & on 19th "C" orders were received for "C" Battery to join 2nd Army Artillery School. Further particulars & Training orders. Their rifle was carried out on 1st inst.	

Army Form C. 2118.

162ND BRIGADE,
ROYAL
FIELD ARTILLERY.

No. ....
Date ....

WAR DIARY
or
INTELLIGENCE SUMMARY.
(Erase heading not required.)

February 1918.

Instructions regarding War Diaries and Intelligence Summaries are contained in F.S. Regs., Part II. and the Staff Manual respectively. Title pages will be prepared in manuscript.

Place	Date	Hour	Summary of Events and Information	Remarks and references to Appendices
	3/16 1918 Con'd		Major I.C. Hill, M.C., O.C Battery was also instructed to join 1st Army Artillery School at VAUX-EN-AMIENOIS as an instructor. He left on 19th inst. During his absence O/162 was temporarily commanded by A/Capt M.M. Beatty, M.C., of A/162.	
	20th		The Brigade less C/162 left Rest Area & marched to RENESCURE. En route, Howitzers of B/162 were calibrated at TILQUES, billets for personnel and the Howitzers for night 20/21 being found at ST MARTIN-AU-LAERT. Howitzer Bde on the march next day they rejoined Bde on the march.	
	21st		Bde left RENESCURE & marched to RIEVELD about 4 kilos. south of WORMHOUDT. From here Advance Parties proceeded by rail to VLAMERTINGHE to take over Wagon Lines of 305th Bty.	
	22nd		From RIEVELD the horse lines of 1 Section per battery and pack of Bde Hdrs dunst to forward area. Bde Hdrs took over No.1 Group Hdrs (305th Bde (Bt. Hdrs) + Batn Sections relieving corresponding Section of 305th Bde Batteries in action. Remaining Battery Sections & Wagon lines marched to Wagon Lines – "B" + "D" Batteries and Hdrs about 1 mile S.E. VLAMERTINGHE, "A" Battery about 1 mile West of YPRES just off the main VLAMERTINGHE – YPRES Road.	

Army Form C. 2118.

WAR DIARY
or
INTELLIGENCE SUMMARY.

(Erase heading not required.)

February 1918.

162nd BRIGADE,
ROYAL
FIELD ARTILLERY.

Place	Date	Hour	Summary of Events and Information	Remarks and references to Appendices
	2nd to 20th		Remaining Run line personnel proceeded by lorries to battery positions forward area, from whence they went to gun positions to complete relief of Batteries left 20th Feb 1918.	
	21st – 28th		The Bde in action covered our own Divisional Infantry on a front of about 1000 yds just south of PASSCHENDAELE. Batteries were situated along the LANGEMARCK and ZONNEBEKE Rd. "A" & "D" Batteries 600ˣ N.W of ZONNEBEKE. "B" Battery 2000ˣ NW of ZONNEBEKE. Bde also was in a pill-box about 1000ˣ NE of ZONNEBEKE, FREZENBERG. Since being in action the policy has been to remain quiet only registration and calibration being carried out by Batteries. The enemy has, on the whole, remained quiet. He has on one or two occasions tried to make an advance but without success. He raided on a large scale the Division on our right who captured 1 Officer & 15 O.R. of the raiding party.	

Army Form C. 2118.

102ND BRIGADE, ROYAL FIELD ARTILLERY.

No. ....
Date ....

WAR DIARY
or
INTELLIGENCE SUMMARY.
(Erase heading not required.)

February, 1918.

Instructions regarding War Diaries and Intelligence Summaries are contained in F. S. Regs., Part II. and the Staff Manual respectively. Title pages will be prepared in manuscript.

Place	Date	Hour	Summary of Events and Information	Remarks and references to Appendices
			Casualties.	
			Officers —	
			2/Lieut. S. Hawkins. Joined 9th.	
			2/Lieut. E.W. Saunders. " 9th.	
			2/Lieut. J.C. Mitcheson. " 16th.	
			2/Lieut. W. Sunlihy. " 21st.	
			Lieut. J. White M.C. " 22nd.	
			2/Lieut. R.C. Orthanna. " 26th.	
			Lieut. S. Attenborough. To 33rd DAC 16th.	
			Lieut. E. Gildon. To 156th Bde (3A) Bde.	
			Men. —	
			Battle Casualties — Nil.	
			Admitted to Hospital 18.	
			Discharged from " 9.	
			Posted to Bde. 15.	
			Posted away from Bde. 7.	

R.J. Skinner
Commanding 102 Bde. R.F.A.

Army Form C. 2118.

Original Vol 28

162ND BRIGADE, ROYAL FIELD ARTILLERY.
No...........
Date...........

WAR DIARY
INTELLIGENCE SUMMARY.
(Erase heading not required.)

March 1918.

Instructions regarding War Diaries and Intelligence Summaries are contained in F. S. Regs., Part II. and the Staff Manual respectively. Title pages will be prepared in manuscript.

Place	Date	Hour	Summary of Events and Information	Remarks and references to Appendices
	1st		Brigade still in action in position as taken up 22nd February 1918.	
	27th		"C" Battery left 2nd Army Artillery School at THEQUES & marched to PENESCURE.	
	28th		"C" Battery left PENESCURE marched to GODESWARVELDE.	
	29th		"C" Battery left GODESWARVELDE marched to Waten Area at GOLDFISH CHÂTEAU on the YPRES – VLAMERTINGHE Rd.	
Wytschaete/			One Section of Offrs went into action at BOESTINGHE FARM 1000° West of ZONNEBEKE Church.	
Wytschaete			Remaining two Sections of Offrs went into action.	
			The Brigade was covering the Right Battalion Left Bde who held a front from 3000° due west of MOORSLEDE. South East the Bosche made a big raid at 11pm which was repulsed with heavy losses. After the raid some of enemy prisoners taken. On the 2/3 March Left Battalion raided the Convalies Box S.E. of PASSCHENDAELE in which we raided. No casualties were sustained and as identification secured.	

D. D. & L., London, E.C.
(A6014) Wt. W4771/M2:31 750,000 5/17 Sch. 53 Forms/C2118/14

Original Army Form C. 2118.

March 1918.

WAR DIARY
or
INTELLIGENCE SUMMARY.

(Erase heading not required.)

Instructions regarding War Diaries and Intelligence Summaries are contained in F. S. Regs., Part II. and the Staff Manual respectively. Title pages will be prepared in manuscript.

Place	Date	Hour	Summary of Events and Information	Remarks and references to Appendices
In the Field (cont.)			Throughout the period the enemy artillery in forward areas has been quiet. Extensive use of H.V. guns on back areas was made on YPRES, VLAMERTINGHE, POPERINGHE, WATOU, ABEELE. Casualties — Officers — Lieut W. HARLEY wounded (Acc) 7th MAJOR G. FETHERSTON, M.C. wounded 11th (returned to duty) 16th Lieut T. E. WINSHURST both 17th Lieut R. ODHAMS to 3rd Army 21st Capt J.V. MACARTNEY-FILGATE. M.C., Ko 5th Army 21th. Men — Killed 2 Wounded 12 (including 1 or 2nd.), Posted to Bde 17, Gets from Bde 8, Admitted to Hospital 12, (Casualties). Discharged to duty from Hospital 5,	

Bonett Capt
Commanding Trench Mortar Bty, C.C.R.A.

33rd Divisional Artillery.

162nd BRIGADE R.F.A. ::: APRIL 1918.

P/a with 162nd Brigade R.F.A. War Diary for April 1918.

Sheet
33rd Div
Original
J.C. 29

102nd Brigade R.F.A. WAR DIARY or INTELLIGENCE SUMMARY

Army Form C. 2118.

APRIL 1918.

(Erase heading not required.)

Place	Date	Hour	Summary of Events and Information	Remarks and references to Appendices
	1st		Bde still in action in positions as enumerated in March War Diary.	
	7th		Batteries 102 Bde Aly in the line relieved by 281 A.F.A.Bde. Gun line covered withdraws to Wagon line S.E. of VLAMERTINGHE.	
	9th		Bde ordered to move N. of POPERINGHE, "A" & "B" sub to PESELHOEK, "B" to HAMMOCK (at jnxxxx) BOMBEEK xxxxx.	
	10th		Bde ordered to reinforce 30th Division IX Corps. Marched to BRANDHOEK via POPERINGHE. RENINGHELST & LOCRE starting at 2pm.	
	11th		Battery went into action on both banks of roadway along KEMMEL — WERNSTRAAT Road. HQ established in FARM 1 South WERNSTRAAT.	
			Batteries heavily shelled throughout the day by H.V. guns. Many German aeroplanes flew over.	
	12th		HQ moved but two had gone back.	
			O.C. has been ordered to CANADA CORNER & "B" CANADA CORNER. H. LOCRE. "D" has been ordered to RESEXES at MILLEKRUISE CORNER S.W. of SUCKELBUSCH.	
	14th		Sub divisions every attack was pushed to our batteries "A" & "C" S.E. of MILLEKRUISE CORNER xxx "B" "D" MILLEKRUISE. HQ moved 100 yds SE of LOCRE ROUTE.	
	15th		Continual enemy attack in area of DEVONSHIRE xxx now SOUTH E. of BRIGADE "B" "C" South of RENINGHELST, H "D" xxx 1 South NW of RENINGHELST.	
	16th		Calls have had to move from corps to xxxxxxxxxx xxxx xxxx xxxx xxxxx xxxx RENINGHELST. Ordered to xxx forward Wagon lines to MILLEKRUISE xxxxx.	

Original

162 Brigade R.H.A.

WAR DIARY
INTELLIGENCE SUMMARY

APRIL 1918

Army Form C. 2118.

Place	Date	Hour	Summary of Events and Information	Remarks and references to Appendices
	19th		Mb shelled erratically during night shot drew fire on camp.	
	20th		Moved to new H.Q. S.E. of WINDMILL at RENINGHELST. "B", "C", "D" & HQ Wagon Lines moved to camps in vicinity of Windmill at RENINGHELST. Wagon Line Camps shelled. "C" Wagon Lines sustained some casualties. "B" & HQ Wagon Lines moved to camp 6 RENINGHELST. "C" & "D" Wagon Lines sent to bivouacs in the vicinity. Shelter of Sussex 22nd Corps.	
	22nd		"B" & HQ Wagon Lines moved to MUD FARM on the RENINGHELST – POPERINGHE Road about 2000 yds N.W. of RENINGHELST. Later on in the day "B" & HQ Wagon Lines moved back to Camp 6 RENINGHELST.	
	24th		HQ moved to new H.Q. Pozns opp W. of HALLEBAST CORNER. A.C. & D. Pickets moved forward. "B" & HQ Wagon Lines at Camp 6 RENINGHELST.	
	25th		Enemy attacked. A, B & C Batteries moved back to positions East side of ZEVECOTEN – OUDEROOM Road. HQ moved to 300 yds E. of ZEVECOTEN. A, C, & HQ Wagon Lines moved to LISSENHOEK about 2 miles S. of POPERINGHE. D Wagon Line moved back to Camp 6 & "B" to a place about 1000 yds S.W. of OUDEROOM.	
	26th		HQ shelled out. Moved to Camp 6 RENINGHELST. "C" & "D" Wagon Lines joined remainder of Wagon Lines. Wagon Lines shelled throughout night & at Dawn 27th it was necessary to evacuate the camp. C Wagon Line sustained some casualties to personnel & A.K. horses.	

Army Form C. 2118.

WAR DIARY
INTELLIGENCE SUMMARY.
(Erase heading not required.)

162 Bride RHA

APRIL 1918

Place	Date	Hour	Summary of Events and Information	Remarks and references to Appendices
	2nd		"A" & "D" Sub Bdes. Wagon lines moved N. of POPERINGHE – ABEELE Rd. N. of "STRAND WOOD" of POPERINGHE.	
			"B" & "C" Batteries moved to positions N of & near RED MILL, E. N. E of OUDERDOM, "D" Battery to position East of N of OUDERDOM.	
			HQ moved to DE BRIE FARM.	
	3rd		HQ moved to dugout near DE BRIE FARM. FARM. C Battery (one section) moved to High Grove.	

Sheet 4

162 Bgde BHQ **WAR DIARY** Army Form C. 2118.
or
INTELLIGENCE SUMMARY
(Erase heading not required.)

APRIL 1918

Place	Date	Hour	Summary of Events and Information	Remarks and references to Appendices

Casualties. Officers –

Lieut G.T.S. Clarke pnel 13/4/18.
Major W.A.T. Bowker. DSO. M.C gassed 10/4/18.
Capt T.P. LYSAGHT admitted to hospital remarks 10/4/18.
2/Lieut J.P. Hannon M.C. Wounded 25/4/18
2/Lieut C.A. Squires. Killed 25/4/18.
2/Lieut G. Saunders. Wounded 25/4/18.
2/Lieut R.C. Rose. Wounded 29/4/18
2/Lieut R.G. Garrat. Wounded at Duty 25/4/18.

Men

Battle Casualties –
{ Killed 17.
94 { Died of Wounds 4.
   { Wounded 57.
   { Gassed 8.
   { Wounded at Duty 8.

Admitted to Hospital 16 (all accounts)
Discharged from hospital to Duty 5.
Posted to Bde 27.
" from " 6.

E.J. Shannon Lieut C/162 BHQ
C/162 Bde HQ BH.

NOTE ON ACTIVITIES OF 162nd BDE.R.F.A. SENT BY COLONEL E.J. SKINNER

23/2/53

162nd Brigade R.F.A. 1918

16th April

The 162nd Brigade was in action N.E. of Kemmel Village in the area between Rossignol Wood - Parret Camp in positions which had been occupied on 12th April. The brigade H.Q. was in Parret Camp, a Nissen hut camp on the Kemmel - Vierstraat road, which was at that time empty. The batteries were sited to fire on a very big arc and were kept busy. The whole area in which they were in action was subjected to heavy bursts of fire every day. Kemmel Hill was constantly shelled, principally it seemed by 5.9" howitzers.

The early morning of 16th April was foggy and at first visibility was poor but it improved later. No indication of any attack was received, such as a preliminary barrage or a bombardment of the batteries. There was only the usual daily shelling. The enemy moved forward in the mist and reached the O.P. area and it was then that the first real information was received of an attack. The advance seemed to be from Lindhoek in a N.W. direction. Kemmel Hill was heavily shelled and one had the impression that, as an obvious O.P. it was being blinded. Visibility had improved as the morning wore on and the batteries were heavily shelled. It seemed apparent that the Germans had moved forward a number of field batteries.

As the enemy continued to advance and the ranges of the batteries decreased - they were now firing at ranges under 1,000 yards - the brigade was ordered to retire. The retirement was carried out by sections and the batteries came into action E. of the Millekruisse - Hallebast Corner road, between the road and the Kemmel Beck. The O.P's were in the area vacated by the guns. When the enemy advance reached a line approximately 1,000 yards from the Kemmel - Vierstraat road and parallel to it, east of Rossignol Wood,

it stopped. There was no immediate counter-attack that day
and the rest of the day passed off quietly. During the night
16/17th April, the brigade H.Q., which were in some broken
down buildings in front of the centre of the batteries, was
heavily shelled and suffered considerable casualties. There
seemed to be no particular reason for this burst of hostile
fire. It was symptomatic of the heavy bursts of shelling
to which various localities were subjected during this period.
On the morning of the 17th the Brigade H.Q. moved to Millekruisse.

17th - 24th April

There was the usual shelling of the area, particularly
heavy on the 17th. The Germans made no noticeable advance,
and remained more or less on the line reached on the 16th.
There were some local counter-attacks on our part which were
supported by the batteries, but no great change in the front
resulted. The batteries pressed forward sections to the
neighbourhood of Siege Farm just W. of the Kemmel - Vierstraat
road. The main battery positions were strengthened and
communications improved.

21st April

The brigade was put under the command of the French 28th
Division. The brigade H.Q. moved to Scherpenberg to be with
the French H.Q., the batteries remaining in their positions.
This was an inconvenient arrangement on account of the long
lateral communications from the brigade H.Q. to the batteries,
and on 24th April the Brigade H.Q. returned to Millekruisse,
where there was no the H.Q. of the officer commanding a
"Groupe" of artillery of the French 28th Division. This
"Groupe" was in action to the right rear of the 162nd Brigade,
E. of Millekruisse.

24th April.

Was a particularly quiet day. The only shelling was the deliberate and careful registration by the enemy of various points in the battery areas, such as battery positions and road junctions. This registration, which was reported to 9th Divisional H.Q., was most obvious. It was presumably carried out by air observation. The enemy's balloons had moved up very close, and in addition his aeroplanes were most aggressive. In this area they certainly completely outnumbered our aeroplanes and flew calmly, and low down, over all the area.

General Observations

(1).   Good Spring weather prevailed during the period. There was generally mist in the early morning which cleared away as the sun grew stronger. The going was good.

(2).   The French divisions had come from Alsace where they apparently had a very quiet life. The officers of the 28th French Division, to which the 162nd Brigade was attached, constantly remarked on the difference in the amount of fire between their present position and Alsace, where, they said, the arrival of a hostile bullet used to be reported!

At Kemmel the French 28th Division suffered very heavy casualties, especially on the road from La Clytte to Kemmel, which was constantly full of their troops going up or coming from the line. Their dead lay everywhere and I think this had a very dispiriting effect on them.

(3).   Air. There is no doubt at this period the enemy had complete command of the air in the Kemmel area. Their aeroplanes flew constantly over battery positions and their balloons were moved very close to the line. This was most noticeable on the 24th April.

Original
Sheet 1
Vol 30

Army Form C. 2118.

162nd BRIGADE
R.F.A.
No ....
Date ....

WAR DIARY
INTELLIGENCE SUMMARY
(Erase heading not required.)

Place	Date	Hour	Summary of Events and Information	Remarks and references to Appendices
	1st		Brigade still in action in position as stated in April War Diary	
	8th		Wagon lines moved to WINNEZEELE	
	9th		Brigade relieved in action by 121 Bde R.F.A. — marches direct to WINNEZEELE	
	12th		Brigade left WINNEZEELE to go into action in II Corps area, 17th Bde R.F.A. were relieved as follows — A/162 relieved 13th Bty. B/162 " 26th Bty. C/162 " 92nd Bty. D/162 " 9th Bty. A/162 R.H. " A/172 R.H. AL/162 All Batteries & Headquarters located in vicinity of SALVATION CORNER, YPRES. Wagon lines were about 3050 yards E.N.E. of POPERINGHE near the main POPERINGHE — ELVERDINGHE Road. Bde came under the orders of 29th Divl Arty.	
	16th		One section per battery relieved in action by corresponding section of Batteries of 17th Bde R.H.A. Hor de Nord withdrawn to wagon lines.	
	17th		Remaining battery sections of Bde also relieved by corresponding sections of Btys of 17th Bde R.H.A. withdrawn to Wagon lines.	
	18th		Brigade marched to + took over wagon lines vacated by 122 Bde R.F.A. in fields about 1 mile N.E. of HOUTKERQUE.	

Original

Army Form C. 2118.
Sheet 2.

162nd BRIGADE,
R.F.A.

No ....
Date ....

May 1918

WAR DIARY
INTELLIGENCE SUMMARY.
(Erase heading not required.)

Instructions regarding War Diaries and Intelligence Summaries are contained in F. S. Regs., Part II. and the Staff Manual respectively. Title pages will be prepared in manuscript.

Place	Date	Hour	Summary of Events and Information	Remarks and references to Appendices
	18th to 30th		This period was spent in rest & training. A reconnaissance was made of Reserve Battery Positions & Obs Stns to be occupied in case of attack to support the English Division that would support the right of the Belgian Army. All 18-pdrs were re-calibrated at ALQUES Calibration Range by 22nd Sound Ranging Section on the 29th inst. Obs Stns (concrete structures) were built at 2/62 Wagon Lines.	
	31st.		Orders received to relieve 246th Bde RFA, 49th Div Art, who were covering part of the YPRES Sector on nights 1/2 & 2/3 June 1918.	

Original

Army Form C. 2118.
Sheet 3

May 1918.

WAR DIARY
or
INTELLIGENCE SUMMARY.
(Erase heading not required.)

162nd BRIGADE,
R.F.A.
No ....
Date ....

Place	Date	Hour	Summary of Events and Information	Remarks and references to Appendices
			Casualties.	
			Officers.	
			Lieut-Col. E.C. Oldham joined 13th. Lieut R.C. Esson December 24/4/1918	
			2/Lieut R.S. Reid " 12th. Lieut J Sherman 14/5/1918 }	
			Lieut C.R. Vaughan-Hughes " " Lieut-Col. E.J. Sherman D.S.O. to	
			2/Lieut R.A.S. Maclin " 22nd. England sick 9/5/1918.	
			2/Lieut M.N. Anderson " " 2/Lieut R.G. Grover Wounds 2/5/1918.	
			2/Lieut W.K. Shaw " 27th. 2/Lieut S.H. McDonnell } to 12 D.R.S.	
			Lieut J.G.S. Chapman " 31st. 2/Lieut C.J. Moore } 15/5/1918	
			2/Lieut M.A. Rumbles " 7th. 2/Lieut J.S. Gilbert to England sick 15/5/1918	
			Lieut J. Gould M.C. to Latrine Corps Base	
			Spr 13/5/1918.	
			Other Ranks.	
			Battle Casualties - { Killed & Died of Wounds 10.	
			Wounded 28 (including 6 remaining at duty.)	
			Postings. To Brigade 154.	
			From Brigade 15.	
			Hospital. Admissions — 38. (including 20 wounded.)	
			Discharge to duty — 11.	

J.E. Wilson
Comdg 162 Brigade R.F.A. Lieut-Col R.A.

Army Form C. 2118.

WAR DIARY
or
INTELLIGENCE SUMMARY.
(Erase heading not required.)

102ND BRIGADE ROYAL FIELD ARTILLERY.

Ja 31

Place	Date	Hour	Summary of Events and Information	Remarks and references to Appendices
	June 1st & 2nd		Relief of 246th Bde RFA 49th Div Ank. One section per battery marched to new wagon lines on 1st went into action night 1st/2nd. Remaining sections and Bde HQrs marched to new wagon line on 2nd & went into action night 2nd/3rd. HQrs took up for HQrs 246th Bde RFA at a farm about 4000 yds W.S.W of YPRES. HQrs wagon line were situated N.W of BRANDHOEK & about 800 yds north of the main POPERINGHE — VLAMERTINGHE Road. Batteries relieved corresponding batteries of 246th Bde RFA in action West of and at distances varying from 3500 yds to 3800 yds from YPRES. A Bde was the Right Battalion Bde Infantry Bde opposite VOORMEZEELE. B/162 about 800 yds N of HAMHOEK, C/162 in the main battery wagon lines were situated — A/162 about 800 yds N of HAMHOEK, B/162 in the wood South East of VOX VRIE farm, road of the POPERINGHE — WOESTEN Road, C/162 about 500 yds N of STEENJE CABT on the POPERINGHE — ELVERDINGHE Rd, D/162 near HQ wagon lines. A B + C/162 established forward Wagon lines in the vicinity + N.W of VLAMERTINGHE.	
	4th		B/162 wagon lines moved back to a place 400 yds S.W of the point where the CANAL POPERINGHE branch the POPERINGHE — WOESTEN Rd, leaving forward wagon lines where their main wagon line had been.	

Army Form C. 2118.

162ND BRIGADE,
ROYAL
FIELD ARTILLERY.
No............
Date............

WAR DIARY
or
INTELLIGENCE SUMMARY.
(Erase heading not required.)

Place	Date	Hour	Summary of Events and Information	Remarks and references to Appendices
	JUNE 5th		Men shelled out and also then established in old horse standings on the OUDEZEELE – VLAMERTINGHE Road. 250 yds S.W. of VLAMERTINGHE. Men Wagon lines moved back to vicinity of B/162 wagon lines.	
	6th			
	8th		Battery fired in support of Durnal attack on RIDGE & SCOTTISH Woods. Attack was unsuccessful.	
	10th		C/162 moved our dug-in position 500 yards West into some old horse standings.	
	11th		Men B.C. on the M.S. of ISTEL Bu Rd in a bay from 300 yds S.W. of VLAMERTINGHE.	
	13th		Battery again fired in support of Durnal attack on RIDGE & SCOTTISH Woods. 200 hrs at W.How. Attack was again unsuccessful.	
			A C.& D. Patrols fired in other quiet moved out by midnight by M/1 VLAMERTINGHE. Raiding party come in contact with a similar raiding party of the enemy and many killed. The pass on pursuing was taken. R/162 Battery fires a complete fresh around at N. Mouse gas pursuing round of ZILLEBEKE LAKE. Raiding party again their shelled and LM.G. Fire.	

Army Form C. 2118.

WAR DIARY
or
INTELLIGENCE SUMMARY.
(Erase heading not required.)

102ND BRIGADE,
ROYAL
FIELD ARTILLERY.

Place	Date	Hour	Summary of Events and Information	Remarks and references to Appendices
	JUNE			
	25/26th	10.45 am	C/50 was successfully discharged from BEDFORD HOUSE south of YPRES.	
	26/27th		Batteries fired in co-operation. Harassing fire was carried out during the night on communications & selected targets.	
	26/27th		6th English Division relieved 11th Durham Division on our right.	
	27/28th	3.10 am	Gas fire & chemical barrage on NOORDEMZEELE.	
	28th		Hun's C.B. again very heavy & made task of the hundred yards owing to prematures & enemy fire over shelling. B/162 sustaining some casualties.	
	28/29th		Brigade established a field Listening Station between 11.30pm & 12.30am in co-operation with a raid carried out by 146th Division on our left.	
	30/1st		11th Army Bde RA left the area & Bde covered 11th & 14th Right Infantry Bdes, 146th(?) Division A covering the left.	

Army Form C. 2118.

WAR DIARY
or
INTELLIGENCE SUMMARY.
(Erase heading not required.)

102ND BRIGADE,
ROYAL
FIELD ARTILLERY,
No..........
Date..........

Instructions regarding War Diaries and Intelligence Summaries are contained in F. S. Regs., Part II. and the Staff Manual respectively. Title pages will be prepared in manuscript.

Place	Date	Hour	Summary of Events and Information	Remarks and references to Appendices

Casualties.

Officers.

14. Capt J.H. Harris M.C. from 59th Bde to command A/I.S Sec 161 BdeHQ

9th Major W.A.T. Bowman 2nd in C. OHD wounded (Right thigh) 33th Bgn Ak
10th Lieut A.E. Anderson posted to B/162 from Res.
15th Lieut R.V. B.F. Hallam to hospital
Lieut-Col R.E. Kennedy O.S.O. posted to command Bde.
17th Major J.L. Lee M.C. YMD to return to Coursche from D Ak.
Major R.E. Rowell posted from D/162 Bde. (B) to command Bde.

Men.

Rank Casualties — { Killed 2.
{ Wounded 10 (including 3 remaining at duty).
Sick { Admitted to Hospital 30.
     { Remained to Duty 24.
At Duty 14.
Rejoined 20.
Posted { to Bde 10.
       { from Bde 16.

R. Kennedy Lieut Colonel RA
Commanding 102 Bde R.F.A.

162 B[de] RFA Appx
Vol 32

WAR DIARY
INTELLIGENCE SUMMARY

Army Form C. 2118.

JULY 1918.

162ND BRIGADE, ROYAL FIELD ARTILLERY.

Place	Date	Hour	Summary of Events and Information	Remarks and references to Appendices
	JULY 1st		Battery in action and wagon lines in same position as enumerated in JUNE War Diary.	
	2/3rd night	12.5am	'A' & 'B' Batteries assisted in a Chinese Barrage on the left Infantry Bde Front. Bgde Ran war' at 12.5am and Barrage lasted until 12.38am.	
	5/6th night	11.15pm	At 11.15pm a raid was carried out by the 9th H.L.I. 100th Infantry Bde on a trench between VOORMEZEELE and LOCK 8 on the Canal bank. O.C. Bde made all arrangements for the Artillery support. Owing to Infantry being late in forming up and rapidity of enemy reply to our barrage tychis were not gained.	
	14th	6am	At 6am 2 companies of the 1st Middlesex Regt., with the 18th Infantry Bde 6th Division on their right attacked in order to re-establish our line at RIDGE WOOD & in front of VOORMEZEELE. The attack was a complete success over 320 prisoners being captured. Some 18pdr batteries opened fire 5 minuts too early but from all accounts the barrage was good. 3 minuts after our barrage started the enemy's barrage came down on our front & support lines. At first the fire was fairly heavy but slackened after about 15 mins to and then again became heavy for a further 10 minuts. At no time was it really strong & effective. The enemy did not attempt to leaving on our left until 20 mins after the commencement of the barrage. Throughout the day there was considerable Trench Mortar activity and movement was observed by the F.O.O. enabling the batteries to make some very good shooting. Enemy fire during the day consisted of hurricane bursts in the area captured.	

WAR DIARY

INTELLIGENCE SUMMARY.

(Erase heading not required.)

Army Form C. 2118.

162ND BRIGADE, ROYAL FIELD ARTILLERY.

JULY 1918.

Place	Date	Hour	Summary of Events and Information	Remarks and references to Appendices
	JULY			
	Night 14th/15th	12 M.N. 2.45 am	At 12 midnight and again at 2.45am the Brigade fired Counter-Preparation.	
	14th-16th		5 American Infantry Officers were attached to the Bde to learn the methods of the Artillery. One was attached to each Battery and one to Bde.	
	16/7th		Bde co-operated with "Hanto" in bombardment of VOORMEZEELE & ST ELOI.	
	17th		Bonnet sights of 'C' Battery heavily shelled. Both guns were "knocked out".	
	Night 17th/18th		Bde fired Counter Preparation.	
	Night 21st/22nd		Bde fired Counter Preparation.	
	Night 22nd/23rd		Bde fired Counter Preparation.	
	23/7/18		An American battalion of the 30th American Division took over the left Battalion front Right Infantry Brigade.	
	30th		Brig-Genl. C.G. Stewart, C.M.G., D.S.O., R.A., B/ C the Divisional Artillery Command was taken over by Brig-Genl. G.H.W. Nicholson C.M.G., R.A.	

Army Form C. 2118.

WAR DIARY
—or—
INTELLIGENCE SUMMARY.
(Erase heading not required.)

162ND BRIGADE, ROYAL FIELD ARTILLERY.
No..................
Date................

July 1918

Place	Date	Hour	Summary of Events and Information	Remarks and references to Appendices
			Casualties.	
			(a) Officers.	
			2/Lt. E.T.G. Donovan joins Bde + posted to "A" Bty 8/7/18.	
			2/Lt. H.L.W. Hughes joins Bde + posted to "C" Bty 17/7/18.	
			2/Lt. W.K. Shaw admitted to Hospital 11/7/18.	
			Lt. A.K. Henderson admitted to Hospital whilst on Course at TIQUES 27/7 – 5/8	
			(b) Men.	
			Battle Casualties – { 1 Died of Wounds	
			{ 9 Wounded	
			12. { 2 Wounded at Duty.	
			Hospital – { Admitted 15. (8 evacuated)	
			{ Discharged to Duty 10.	
			Posted – { To Bde 22.	
			{ From Bde 8.	

H. Rawcliffe Lieut. Colonel R.A.
O.C. 162nd Brigade R.F.A.

162nd Brigade R.F.A. Army Form C. 2118.

WAR DIARY
or
INTELLIGENCE SUMMARY.

(Erase heading not required.)

August 1918.

Place	Date	Hour	Summary of Events and Information	Remarks and references to Appendices
	1st.		Brigade in action in positions as last enumerated in July War Diary.	
	2nd.		6th Division on our right raided the enemy's lines at the BRASSERIE, south of VOORMEZEELE. Zero was 7.5 am. "C"/162 and 2 Howitzers of D/162 assisted by putting up a flank smoke screen on the S.E. of VOORMEZEELE. The raid was a complete success 4 prisoners being obtained and valuable information. The prisoners belonged to the 8th Division.	
	3rd/4th		174th Brigade 39th Div. Arty withdrew to their wagon lines. They had been covering the Left Infantry Brigade. We took over their "S.O.S" lines and 156th Brigade R.F.A., took over the whole of the Right Infantry Brigade front. Our front was extended from just south of ZILLEBEKE LAKE to the canal. The 4th King's Regiment attempted to make a silent raid on BLAUWE POORT FARM. The Brigade stood by ready to co-operate if required, the signal for such action to be a rocket sent up by the raiding party. The latter reached their objectives but found no signs of the enemy and withdrew safely to our lines without casualties.	
	7th/8th		The rear position of A/162 was moved to a position of the 49th Div. Arty 500 yards N.E., of GOLDFISH CHATEAU midway between VLAMERTINGHE and YPRES.	
	8th.		Capt. Fields of the 30th American Divisional Artillery was attached to the Brigade for instruction. He left on the 22nd.	
	9th.		The Brigade fired in co-operation of a bombardment by field and heavy artillery on VOORMEZEELE.	
	10th.		C/162 moved to a position next to that taken up by A/162 in the vicinity of GOLDFISH CHATEAU.	
	20th.		The Brigade fired in co-operation with Heavy Artillery II Corps in a bombardment of LANKHOF CHATEAU AND CAMP and of LA CHAPELLE.	
	24th.		The Brigade fired in co-operation with Heavy Artillery II and XIX Corps in a bombardment of ROZARIE FARM and PICCADILLY FARM.	

Army Form C. 2118.

WAR DIARY
or
INTELLIGENCE SUMMARY.
(Erase heading not required.)

162nd Brigade R.F.A.,   **August 1918.**

Place	Date	Hour	Summary of Events and Information	Remarks and references to Appendices
	Night/27th.		A Gas Cloud attack was carried out. The Brigade co-operated with harassing fire on dug-outs etc.,	
	Nights 29/30 & 30/31st		The Brigade was relieved in action by 331st Brigade R.F.A., 66th D.A., withdrew to wagon lines and from thence marched to camps near HOUTKERQUE. The billets were the same as those occupied by the Brigade in May 1918.	
	31st		Orders received about 12.30 am for Brigade to move to G.H.Q. reserve Third Army Area.	
	Night 31st/ 1/9/1918 & 1/9/1918		Batteries and Headquarters marched indepently to entraining stations at WAAYENBURG and HEIDEBEKE, where the Brigade was entrained and proceeded to 3rd Army Area, detraining at PREVENT and BOUQUE MAISON on 1-9-1918. From these stations the Brigade marched to and concentrated in billets at in the vicinity of BROUILLY CHATEAU, near HEBREUVIERE and ROZIERE on the main PREVENT - AVESNES LE COMTE Road.	

Alexander Lt Col RFA
Comdg 162 F.A.B.

Army Form C. 2118.

162nd Brigade R.F.A.,

WAR DIARY
or
INTELLIGENCE SUMMARY
(Erase heading not required.)

August 1918.

Place	Date	Hour	Summary of Events and Information	Remarks and references to Appendices
			Casualties –	
			Officers. – Lieut B.S.M.Paterson, Joined 27-8-1918.	
			Capt. J.T.Gorman, To England for tour of duty 29-8-1918.	
			Major M.M.I.Body, To England for tour of duty 31-8-1918.	
			Lieut A.E.Henderson, granted 3 weeks sick leave by Medical Board at BOULOGNE, and struck off strength 14-8-1918.	
			Capt A.Heads, M.C., posted from D/156 Bde R.F.A., 29-8-1918.	
			Lieut R.C.Norton, Admitted to hospital 4-8-1918.	
			Other ranks. –	
			Posted to Bde. 36.	
			Posted from Bde 14.	
			Admissions to Hospital 27.	
			Discharges from hospital 14.	
			Battle Casualties 2 O.R's Wounded.	
	2-9-1918.			

O.R.Cawthra
Lieut-Colonel R.F.A.,
Commanding 162nd Brigade R.F.A.,

September 1918. War Diary.   Original. 1
                                                                  162 Bde RFA

162 Bde RFA / 33 Div

4th. Bde remained at ROZIERE. Whenever weather conditions permitted tactical schemes & training were carried out. On the 5th a Div'l Arty parade was held & inspected by Major-General PINNEY (G.O.C. Division). The Bde co-operated in a Divisional Tactical scheme with the Infantry on 11th, open positions being taken up & advances made as in open warfare. Owing to the wet this was done in skeleton order. Guns were calibrated at 3rd Army Calibration Range FROHEN-LE-GRAND on the 4th, 5th, 6th & 7th.

9th Lieut Col R.G. Ramsden D.S.O. was admitted to Hospital. Major G. Fetherston M.C., A/162 took over Bde command.

Night 14/15 8pm. Bde marched to LOUVENCOURT arriving about 5 am (22 miles)

" 15/16 8pm. Bde marched to LE TRANSLOY via ACHEUX.

16th. 4pm. Bde marched to BUS & established Wagon Lines. Batteries & HQrs moved into action about 1000ˣ N. of HEUDICOURT.

17th Registration carried out by batteries. Wagon line areas heavily shelled. This continued nightly up to the end of the month.

18th Bde supported an attack on CHAPEL HILL & GAUCHE WOOD. Zero hour 5.20 am. Attack very successful on immediate front. Division on left held up. A large number of prisoners were taken & guns ~~taken~~ captured.

19th Major A Barker D.S.O., M.C., posted from C/162 to command Bde.

20th

21st Batteries supported an attack by the 33rd Div'l Infantry on their right putting down a creeping Barrage during the operation at 5.40am. Wagon Lines moved up from BUS to the area just West of EQUANCOURT.

22nd

23rd. Bde & Batteries moved forward to new positions about 2000ˣ S.S.E. Advanced guns moving up in the afternoon were subject to heavy enemy fire. During the night HQrs & B/162 were gassed, the whole personnel becoming casualties. Major G. Fetherston M.C., A/162 took over command at midnight & commanded the Bde from his Battery Position.
A bomb which fell in C/162's Wagon Lines killed 2, wounded 4 ORs & destroyed all Q.M. Sh stores.

Appendix 2

24th. Morning fine cleared [up?] by all B.C.s [?] [?] [?] [?].
A/162 moved one gun into an advanced position from which
large areas of enemy country could be commanded over [open?]
sights.

25th. Owing to shortage of Officers, Major [?] guns of B/162 were
transferred one to 'A' one to 'C'.
A day of much local fire [?] [?] [?] hostile battery
counter fire [?] to the batteries.

26. 4 Canvas [?] [?] were attached to batteries 2 to A +
2 to C/162 — a supply of enemy yellow cross shell, which was
[?] against him during the night [?] [?] being expended.
Casualties A/162 2 ORs Killed, 4 ORs Wounded. Lieut. [?]
Hadley C/162 Wounded.

27th. Roads + approaches to VILLERS GUISLAIN heavily shelled during the
night. D/162 fired concentrated bursts of gas shell on HONNECOURT
WOOD
400 7.7cm mustard gas shell were fired into enemy lines.

28th. Battery Commanders all reconnoitred forward areas with a view to
moving up batteries in the event of coming operations proving
successful.

29th. Bde supported attack on VILLERS GUISLAIN by 98th Inf/Bde at
3.30am + on the trenches East at 5.30am. Progress made by the
Infantry very irregular, + the day developed into one long hard fight,
all batteries being heavily engaged.
At 2pm 'B + C' Batteries moved forward to positions 1500's SW
of VILLERS GUISLAIN [?] [?] [?] [?] fire enroute +
being subject later to concentrated shell fire from 4.2" +
7.7cm. During their advance 'A + D' batteries dealt with
enemy movement + attempted counter attacks N. of VILLERS
GUISLAIN.

30th. the enemy having retired during the night A/162 moved into
position W. of VILLERS GUISLAIN and [?] 30/hr. [?]
batteries moved forward about 1000' E of VILLERS GUISLAIN

Summary.

Original 3

Casualties.   (1). Officers.

Lieut-Col R.B. Ramsden DSO, admitted to Hospital 9th.
To England 19th - struck off strength.

2/Lieut J.C. Mitcheson. D/162 Wounded 16th,

2/Lieut H.J. Cholderott posted from Base 11th, Wounded for duty 18th (To Hospital - 1/10/18),
Major G. Fetherston M.C.
Major A. Barker DSO, M.C. posted from D/156 14th,

Major A. Barker DSO, M.C. ⎫
Major H.C. Cory, M.C.   ⎪
Capt R.H. Pavitt   ⎪
Capt G. Coleman   ⎬ Wounded (Gas)
Lieut B.S. McC. Paterson ⎪   28/9/18.
Lieut H.J.R. Couth   ⎪
2/Lieut T.E. Winnehurst   ⎪
2/Lieut M.H. Rollason   ⎭

2/Lieut P.A.S. Hadley. Wounded 27-9-18,

Major M.A.L. Body, M.C., to England for tour of duty 31-8-18,
Capt. A. Heads M.C., posted from D/156 29-8-18,

(2). Men

Battle Casualties ⎧ Killed - 3., Died of Wounds .. 1.
                  ⎨ Wounded - 17,
                  ⎪ Wounded (Gas) - 65,
                  ⎩ Wounded at duty 4

⎧ Admitted to Hospital 24
⎩ Discharged to duty from Hospital 9.

⎧ Posted to Bde 36.
⎩ Posted from Bde 5.

Summary.

Army Form C. 2118.

162nd Brigade. R.F.A.

Instructions regarding War Diaries and Intelligence
Summaries are contained in F. S. Regs., Part II.
and the Staff Manual respectively. Title pages
will be prepared in manuscript.

WAR DIARY
or
INTELLIGENCE SUMMARY.
(Erase heading not required.)

OCTOBER 1918.

Place	Date	Hour	Summary of Events and Information	Remarks and references to Appendices
	1st	3.30	Batteries still in position 1000 yards E. of VILLERS GUISLIAN. 7 a.m. Batteries put down a Barrage in support of an Infantry attack on VILLERS GUISLIAN. All Batteries were subjected to area straafs put down by the enemy to cover his retreat.	
	3rd.		The Brigade advanced at Dawn to positions nearer E. of VILLERS GUISLIAN and fired into HONNECOURT - Good Targets presented themselves on the opposite side of the CANAL where much movement was seen.	
	6th		Brigade crossed the CANAL by the Lock in S.13 b. at about 6 p.m. having had to wait 3 or 4 hours for Bridges to be constructed and then came into action in the HINDENBURG LINE in the vicinity of FRASQUE WOOD and LA TERRIEE.	
	7th		Batteries moved forward to BASKET WOOD East of the Hindenburg Line. Wagon Lines moved to Canal Bank in the vicinity of TARGELLE VALLEY.	
	8th		Barrage put down by the Batteries in support of Infantry attack at 1 a.m. Batteries moved forward to N. of MOSCHO WOOD from which a further Barrage was fired at 11 a.m.	
	9th	1 a.m.	Information received that the 34th Infantry Brigade would be prepared to advance with the object of securing the crossings of the LA SELLE CANNAL and establishing positions in high ground in N.16 and X.13. Information received that the enemy was falling back and that the front was only slightly held - orders were issued for the advance to be continued on the morning of the 12th instant. The Brigade advanced after the BOSCHE all day and passed through VILLERS OUTREAUX, MALINCOURT, ELINCOURT, CLARY and on the BERTRY in the vicinity of which the night was spent. CLARY AND BERTRY were both in occupation by French Civilians who gave the British Troops a hearty welcome. During the course of the Day the Batteries were in action three times and fired at the request of the Infantry to support their advance. Wagon Lines experienced considerable difficulty in keeping in touch with the Battery Gun Lines and also in keeping up with the advance - but after a long days march they joined their firing Batteries in the vicinity of BE TRY.	

Army Form C. 2118.

WAR DIARY
or
INTELLIGENCE SUMMARY.

(Erase heading not required.)

Instructions regarding War Diaries and Intelligence Summaries are contained in F. S. Regs., Part II. and the Staff Manual respectively. Title pages will be prepared in manuscript.

Place	Date	Hour	Summary of Events and Information	Remarks and references to Appendices
	10th		Firing Batteries march at dawn and the enemy were found to be in strength on the opposite side of the LA SELLE RIVER. Batteries marched through TROISVILLES and came into action N. of the LE CHATEAU ROAD. Teams were shelled heavily whilst bringing the Guns into action and the Battery positions were made very uncomfortable during the day by hostile fire. Brigade Headquarters were established in a House in TROISVILLES. Registration was carried out and a Barrage put down at 5 p.m. in support of our Infantry who were going to cross the LA SELLE RIVER. A very unpleasant night was spent by the Batteries who were without cover on any discription. Wagon Lines remained near BERTRY and Forward Battery Wagon Lines were formed near TROISVILLES.	
	12th		The Infantry attacked without an Artillery Barrage. Batteries were very busy all day harassing the enemy and assisting in repelling Counter Attacks. Orders were received that the 100th Infantry Brigade were to renew the attack at 1700 hrs. Objective - line of road K.22 b.7.8. - K.17 c.1.6. K.10 d.6.0. - Cross Roads K.10 b.5.6. Howitzers to engage Railway embankment with steady fire from receipt of the Orders to Zero Hour i.e., 1700 hrs.	
	15th.		D/162 (Howitzers) co-operated in a bombardment of the Railway in K.9 and K.16. from 4.30 - 4.50.	
	16th		Bombardment as for 15th repeated from 3.25 - 3.45a.m.	
	16/17th		"A"/162 co-operated in a Gas Bombardment on the RAVINE in K.16 a and b.	
	17th.		Brigade co-operated in an attack by the Fourth Army by assisting the 66th Division with an Artillery Barrage.	
	21st.		Orders received that the advance of the THIRD and FOURTH Armies would be continued on the 22/23rd instant.	

Army Form C. 2118.

WAR DIARY
or
INTELLIGENCE SUMMARY.

(Erase heading not required.)

Instructions regarding War Diaries and Intelligence Summaries are contained in F. S. Regs., Part II. and the Staff Manual respectively. Title pages will be prepared in manuscript.

Place	Date	Hour	Summary of Events and Information	Remarks and references to Appendices
	21st.		Attacked to be carried out by 33rd Division on the Right and 21st Division on the Left. Objective WAGNONVILLE AND POIX-DU-NORD. This Brigade was ordered to detail one Battery of 18 pounders to be placed at the disposal of the G.O.C., 19th Infantry Brigade. The attack was also supported by Tanks.	
	23rd.		Advance continued – Batteries fired a heavy Barrage and stood by xxxxxx until ordered to cross the River LA SELLE.	
		8 a.m.	Batteries came into action in vicinity of K.10 – before they were ready to open fire, it was discovered that the Infantry were out of range – Batteries advanced, and came into action at K.5 at 10.30 a.m. The Infantry were then lining Road running N.E. through L'ABBATTOIR K.25 ready to advance on next objective.	
		12.30 p.m.	Whilst Infantry were advancing Batteries were ordered to move further up and came into action in F. 25 and stood by in case Infantry needed help.	
		3.30 p.m.	Batteries fired bursts of fire in POIX-DU-NORD at the request of the Infantry to neutralise Machine Gun fire.	
	24th	4 a.m.	Batteries put down a Barrage and at day-break a further advance was made – the batteries moving to F.13 – several bursts were fired into the Eastern outskirts of POIX-DU-NORD as the enemy was reported retreating there.	
		8 a.m.	Positions of observation were taken up in F.8 bursts of fire being directed on to the approaches of ENGLEFONTAINE – News was then received that POIX-DU-NORD was clear of the enemy – after a reconnaissance positions were taken up in F.4. During the afternoon the situation as regards ENGLEFONTAINE were not quite clear but the Eastern outskirts of this Town were kept under slow fire.	
	25th	6 a.m.	News was received from the Infantry that they were holding a line half-way between POIX-DU-NORD and ENGLEFONTAINE.	
	26th		Orders were received that the capture of ENGLEFONTAINE was to be completed by the Infantry of 33rd Division – and MT. CARMEL by the 18th Division – 10% Gas shells were used in this attack which was very successful. The 33rd Division (less Artillery) was relieved by 38th Division (less Artillery).	

Army Form C. 2118.

WAR DIARY
or
INTELLIGENCE SUMMARY.
(Erase heading not required.)

Place	Date	Hour	Summary of Events and Information	Remarks and references to Appendices
	28/29th		A Gas Bombardment was put down in the enemy's lines, in which this Brigade assisted.	
	29th	8a.m.	Brigade put down a Barrage in support of Infantry (17th R.W.F) who sent out a raiding party to "Mop" up the House in the ENGLEFONTAINE - BAVAY Road.	
	29/30th		Brigade relieved by the 122nd Brigade. R.F.A. ((38th Division) and marched to Billets in BERTRY for 72 hours rest.	
			The number of Prisoners reported Captured by this Division during the last days Operation Was:- Officers 5 Other Ranks 419.	
			The total number captured by the Division during operations East of the LA SELLE River was:- Officers 23 Other Ranks 1037.	
			Total since 21st September, 1918:- Officers 35 Other Ranks 1673.	
			Lieut.Col: R.F.A. Commanding 162nd Brigade R.F.A.	

Summary of CASUALTIES.

OFFICERS.

Lieut.Col: R.W.R.Warren	Posted from Base.	30.9.18.
2nd Lieut. F. Greenoff	Posted from Base.	1.10.18.
2nd Lieut. S.M. Beall	Posted from Base.	13.10.18.
2nd Lieut. D.W. Flint.	Posted from Base.	7.10.18.
2nd Lieut. G.C. Brown.	Posted from Base.	7.10.18.
2nd Lieut. R. Forbes.	Posted from Base.	7.10.18.
2nd Lieut. E.S. Abbott.	Posted from 21st Div: Sig: Co.	25.9.18.

(Officer i/c., Signal Sub-section R.E. Attached.)

Major G. Fetherston	Wounded (remained at duty) 18.9.18.
	To Hospital 1.10.18.
2nd Lieut. Escott H.J.	Wounded 19.10.18.
2nd Lieut. Shaw W.K.	To England (Sick)"Struck off"
Lieut. Col. Warren W.R.	To Hospital (Sick) 26.10.18.
Lieut. Strachan D.(Adjutant)	To Hospital (Sick) 24.10.18.

OTHER RANKS.

Battn Casualties.

Killed	4
Died of Woundes	2
Wounded	32
Wounded (Gas)	2
Wounded (at duty).	3.

Admitted to Hospital 21.
Discharged from Hospital to duty 1.

Posted to Brigade... ... 86
Posted from Brigade. ... 6.

162nd Brigade. R.F.A.

162 Bde. R.F.A.

Army Form C. 2118.

Instructions regarding War Diaries and Intelligence Summaries are contained in F.S. Regs., Part II. and the Staff Manual respectively. Title pages will be prepared in manuscript.

WAR DIARY
or
INTELLIGENCE SUMMARY.
(Erase heading not required.)

November 1st. 1918.

Place	Date	Hour	Summary of Events and Information	Remarks and references to Appendices
	1st		Brigade still in rest at BERTRY.	
	2nd & 3rd		Brigade in action. Wagon lines at CROIX. (under 38th Div. Artillery) Wagon lines moved to WAGNONVILLE. Gun Line WAGNONVILLE.	
	4th		Colonel E.H.E.Pim wounded. Attack over a wide front. Brigade moved to positions East of ENGLEFONTAIN. Wagon Lines moved to WAGNONVILLE. Major Vaughan Hughes assumed command of the Brigade. Infantry of 33rd Division relieved 38th Division.	
	5th		General advance continued. Brigade moved east of SARBARAS and west of River SAMBRE. The advance was made through the FORET DE MORMAL in extemely wet weather. Wagon lines moved to LOCQUIGNOL.	
	6th		During night and day bridge heads kept under constant shell and machine gun fire. The Brigade was ordered to advance with the infantry across the SAMBRE but was unable to make any progress during the day on account of heavy fire.	
	7th		At dawn Batteries effected a crossing of the SAMBRE RIVER, "D" Battery leading. All Batteries were in action west of POT DE VIN by 10.00 hours. Enemy fire was again very heavy and Batteries suffered many casualties, on account of concentrated fire on roads. Brigade H.Q's remained in close tough with 198th Infantry Brigade in POT DE VIN, and moved forward with Infantry Brigade in the evening to farmhouse 1000 yards east of POT DE VIN. Infantry of 38th Division relieved 33rd Division at 21.00 hours. Wagon Lines moved to SARBARAS.	
	8th		Batteries moved to positions near Cross Roads North West of DOURLERS. At noon Infantry advanced to FAUBEUGE-AVESNES Road and later to BOIS DE BEUGNIES and were supported by our Artillery throughout as far as lay in their power. Wagon lines moved to POT DE VIN area. Since the SAMBRE RIVER was crossed this Brigade(as well as the 169th Army Field Artillery Brigade who were called for on the 7th)was the only Artillery who crossed the River.	
	9th		Enemy commenced a general retirement during the night and early morning and Infantry followed up as far as WATTIGNIES. "B" and "C" Batteries at dawn moved into action 1000 yards West of that village but were not called upon for support. "A" and "D" Batteries with their Wagon	

Army Form C. 2118.

162nd Brigade. R.F.A.

WAR DIARY
or
INTELLIGENCE SUMMARY.
(Erase heading not required.)

Instructions regarding War Diaries and Intelligence Summaries are contained in F. S. Regs., Part II. and the Staff Manual respectively. Title pages will be prepared in manuscript.

Place	Date	Hour	Summary of Events and Information	Remarks and references to Appendices
	9th		Lines moved remained at DOURIERS PENDING further instructions. Brigade H.Q. moved to WATTIGNIES with 113th Infantry Brigade.	
	10th		Wagon lines of "B" and "C" Batteries moved up to the Gun position. Wagon lines of "A" and "D" Batteries were ordered to ECUELIN and TOT DE VTH respectively complete.	
	11th		Hostilities ceased at 11.00 hours. All units of Brigade remained in present positions.	
	12th		Brigade moved from WATTIGNIES to PETIT MAUBEUGE.	
	13th		At PETIT MAUBEUGE.	
	14th		Brigade moved to VENDEGIES-AU-BOIS. Colonel W.R. Warren, D.S.O. rejoined the Brigade from Hospital. Major Vaughan Hughes resumed command of B/162.	
	15th		Brigade moved to CIARY.	
	16th		Brigade moved to IBEDAIN.	
	17th to 20th 22nd		Brigade at IBEDAIN.	
	23rd to 30th 27th		Special Thanksgiving Service attended by Brigade and other Units at GUYNECOUR. C.R.A. presented ribbons to officers and men. Salvage operations commenced. C.R.A. visited the Batteries. Pipe Band Glasgow Highlanders visited Brigade and gave performance.	
	30th		Band performance and Cinema Show by Divisional "Shrapnels"	

Lieut-Col. R.F.A.
Officer Commanding 162nd Bde. R.F.A.

Army Form C. 2118.

162nd Brigade. R.F.A.

162 Bde R.F.A.
Vol 37

Instructions regarding War Diaries and Intelligence
Summaries are contained in F. S. Regs., Part II.
and the Staff Manual respectively. Title pages
will be prepared in manuscript.

WAR DIARY
INTELLIGENCE SUMMARY.
(Erase heading not required.)

December 1918.

Place	Date	Hour	Summary of Events and Information	Remarks and references to Appendices
	1st to 4th		Brigade still billeted at LESDAIN.	
	5th		H.M. King passed through 53rd Divisional Area. Representatives of the Brigade paraded North of CLARY to see the King pass.	
	6th		At LESDAIN.	
	7th		Brigade marched from LESDAIN to MANANCOURT. Billeted for night in Camp recently occupied by Corps Headquarters.	
	8th		Brigade marched to HEAULT, and was billeted for the night under canvas.	
	9th		Brigade marched to PONT NOYELLES.	
	10th		Brigade marched to PICQUIGNY.	
	12th		Brigade marched to ST MAULVIS and remained in billets there until the 12th.	
			Brigade marched as follows:- H.Q. to BEAUCAMP LE VIEUX A/162 INVAL BOIRON. B/162 LEQUESNE. C/162 LE MAZIS. D/162 ST AUBIN RIVIERE.	
	13th to 31st		Brigade remained in above area.	
	14th		General Sir. Reginald Pinney visited Batteries.	
	15th		"A" Battery moved from INVAL BOIRON to BEAUCAMP LE VIEUX.	
	18th		G.O.C.,R.A. 3rd Army visited Batteries.	
	19th &20th		53rd Divisional Band gave two performances	

162nd Brigade. R.F.A.

Army Form C. 2118.

WAR DIARY
or
INTELLIGENCE SUMMARY.

December 1918.

(*Erase heading not required.*)

Instructions regarding War Diaries and Intelligence Summaries are contained in F. S. Regs., Part II. and the Staff Manual respectively. Title pages will be prepared in manuscript.

Place	Date	Hour	Summary of Events and Information	Remarks and references to Appendices
	31st		G.O.C. 53rd Division presented Medal Ribbons to Officers, N.C.O.'s and Men of the Brigade at ST AUBIN RIVIERE.	

[signature]
Lieut-Colonel R.F.A.
Officer Commanding, 162nd Brigade, R.F.A.

162nd BRIGADE, R.F.A.

Army Form C. 2118.

WAR DIARY
or
INTELLIGENCE SUMMARY

JANUARY 1919.

(Erase heading not required.)

Place	Date	Hour	Summary of Events and Information	Remarks and references to Appendices
	1st			
	3rd		Representatives from Brigade attended Lecture by Mr Prior at NEUVILLE on "Influence of Sport on Character."	
	6th		Classification Board visited Batteries and classified Horses with a view to Demobilisation	
	7th		Veterinary Classification of Horses in the Brigade.	
	12th		G.O.C. R.A. 5th Corps visited Batteries.	
			Demobilisation of men in the Brigade commenced.	
	14th		C.R.A. inspected "A" and "B" Batteries.	
			AUMALE Photographer took Group of Brigade Officers.	
	15th		C.R.A. inspected "C" and "D" Batteries.	
	25th		G.O.C. R.A. 3rd Army inspected Batteries.	
	28th		C.R.A. inspected vehicles of each Battery.	
	30th		G.O.C. Division visited "C" and "D" Batteries.	
	31st		184 animals from Brigade sent to No 7 Veterinary Hospital FORGES LES EAU for Demobilisation.	

Captain & Adjutant, R.F.A.
for O.C. 162nd Brigade, R.F.A.

162nd BRIGADE. R.F.A.

Instructions regarding War Diaries and Intelligence
Summaries are contained in F. S. Regs., Part II.
and the Staff Manual respectively. Title pages
will be prepared in manuscript.

WAR DIARY
or
INTELLIGENCE SUMMARY.
(Erase heading not required.)

Army Form C. 2118.

162 Bde R.F.A.

FEBRUARY 1919.

Place	Date	Hour	Summary of Events and Information	Remarks and references to Appendices
	1st to 28th		Nothing of importance to record during month.	
			All Units of Brigade remain in same rest billets.	
	2-3-19			

R.E.W. Hughes
2/Lt for
Captain & Adjutant. R.F.A.
for Officer Commanding, 162nd Brigade. R.F.A.

162nd Brigade. R.F.A.

Army Form C. 2118.

Instructions regarding War Diaries and Intelligence Summaries are contained in F. S. Regs., Part II. and the Staff Manual respectively. Title pages will be prepared in manuscript.

WAR DIARY
or
INTELLIGENCE SUMMARY.
(Erase heading not required.)

MARCH 1919.

Place	Date	Hour	Summary of Events and Information	Remarks and references to Appendices
	1st		All Units of Brigade in same Rest Billets.	
	13th		Brigade reduced to Cadre "A" Establishment. 70 Men Demobilised.	
	15th		104 Animals sent to Remount Depot at Dieppe.	
	18th		37 Animals sent to Remount Depot, ABBEVILLE.	
	24th		Lieut-Colonel Warren, D.S.O. relinquished Command of Brigade.	
	28th		G.O.C., R.A. inspected all Cadres of Brigade and personnel for Army of Occupation.	
	1-4-19			

for Officer Commanding, 162nd Brigade. R.F.A.
Captain & Adjutant. R.F.A.

Army Form C. 2118.

WAR DIARY
INTELLIGENCE SUMMARY
(Erase heading not required.)

162nd Brigade. R.F.A.

APRIL 1919.

Place	Date	Hour	Summary of Events and Information	Remarks and references to Appendices
	1st		Personnel for Army of Occupation concentrated at BEAUCAMP-LE-VIEUX.	
	4th		Brigade moved to Prisoner of War Camp at BLANGY. Horses available for moving vehicles were one pair to each vehicle.	
	7th		All Horses and Mules with the exception of 10 animals per Brigade were sent to Remount Depot, ABBEVILLE.	
	9th		Concert Party from the Lena Ashwell Company at DIEPPE gave Concert at Y.M.C.A. at BLANGY.	
	11th		General Nicholson, Commanding 33rd Division inspected/in Field Service Marching order p men	
	16th		Concert Party from the Lena Ashwell Company at ABBEVILLE gave performance at Y.M.C.A. at BLANGY.	
	24th		R.E. Signal Sub-Section attached to Brigade proceeded to join 33rd Divisional Signal Company.	
	30-4-19			

Captain & Adjutant. R.F.A.
for Officer Commanding, 162nd Brigade. R.F.A.

Army Form C. 2118.

WAR DIARY
or
INTELLIGENCE SUMMARY.

(Erase heading not required.)

162nd Brigade. R.F.A.   MAY. 1919.

Place	Date	Hour	Summary of Events and Information	Remarks and references to Appendices
	1st.		All units of Brigade in P.O.W. Camp? BLANGY.	
	13th to 17th		Further reduction in Cadre Establishment of Brigade. 67 men Demobilised.	

2-6-19

J. Knowles
Captain & Adjutant. R.F.A.
for Officer Commanding, 162nd Brigade. R.F.A.

WAR DIARY
or
INTELLIGENCE SUMMARY

Army Form C. 2118.

162nd Brigade R.F.A.

162 Bde RFA Vol 4 3 erased

Title pages June 1919.

Place	Date	Hour	Summary of Events and Information	Remarks and references to Appendices
	1st.		All units of Brigade in P.O.W. Camp, Blangy.	
	7th.		Cadres of B and C Batteries entrained at Abbeville for England.	
	11th.		Cadres of A and D Batteries, and H.Q. entrained at Abbeville for England.	
	1-7-19			

Latimer
Lieut. and Adjutant, R.F.A.
for Officer Commanding 162nd Brigade R.F.A.

www.ingramcontent.com/pod-product-compliance
Lightning Source LLC
Chambersburg PA
CBHW081531160426
43191CB00011B/1734